C000292104

WRITING AND PUBLISHING YOUR FAMILY HISTORY

Other genealogy titles available from Countryside Books include:

FIRST STEPS IN FAMILY HISTORY
Eve McLaughlin

FURTHER STEPS IN FAMILY HISTORY
Eve McLaughlin

TRACING YOUR ANCESTORS: THE A–Z GUIDE
Pauline Saul

SHORT CUTS IN FAMILY HISTORY
Michael Gandy

DATING OLD PHOTOGRAPHS
Robert Pols

WRITING AND PUBLISHING YOUR FAMILY HISTORY

•••••

JOHN TITFORD

COUNTRYSIDE BOOKS
NEWBURY, BERKSHIRE

First published 1996

COUNTRYSIDE BOOKS
3 Catherine Road
Newbury, Berkshire

ISBN 1 85306 384 3

Designed by Mon Mohan

Produced through MRM Associates Ltd., Reading
Printed by Woolnough Bookbinding Ltd., Irthlingborough.

CONTENTS

●●●●●

(Above, left) Arthur and Annie Buckler, the author's maternal grandparents, on the day of their wedding 1897.
(Above) John Titford graduates from Cambridge University in 1967.
(Left) Doris, Sidney and Harry Titford pose in their Sunday best in the garden of their parents' home in New Southgate, North London, immediately after the First World War.
Do you have a shoe box full of such photographs?

INTRODUCTION

●●●●●

Why would anyone in his or her right mind want to write a family history, let alone publish it? I ought to be dissuading you from doing any such thing. It will cost you a great deal of effort, and could prove very tiring; it could be an expensive undertaking if you want it to be; it could put strains on your relationship with your nearest and dearest; you might not even be happy with the book once you've finished it. Have I dissuaded you? In a world which often seems to be aware of the price of everything and the value of nothing, you might think that only people who really are out of their minds would embark on such an enterprise.

And yet people do it – regularly, and in increasingly large numbers. Why? Here comes the good news. Writing your family history could be one of the most rewarding things you ever do – with rewards measured in terms of personal satisfaction, not financial gain. You may soon discover that there's a book inside you just bursting to get out; with luck you'll tap the deepest springs of your creativity and give the lie to those teachers at school who gave you low marks for English composition. You'll give pleasure to members of your immediate family; your parents and grandparents (if they're still alive) will be proud of you and grateful for what you've done; with luck, distant cousins from all over the globe – cousins you never knew you had – will contact you in gratitude and astonishment at your achievement, be it ever so modest. Perhaps most important of all, you'll feel that you've paid an appropriate and lasting tribute to your ancestors, those individuals who have long since departed this mortal life but have helped to make you what you are. How could you *not* write a family history?

If your cinema-going in recent years has afforded you the chance to see that wonderful film *Dead Poets' Society* starring Robin Williams, you'll know all about the Latin phrase, *carpe diem* – that is, seize the day, grab the opportunity while you can. This could well stand as our text for this book. Without being too morbid about it, we could say that what you intend to do in life, you should start doing today – since none of us has an infinite number of tomorrows, and Time's wingèd chariot appears to have no reverse gear.

My exhortation to you is this: do think seriously about writing your own family history, and do think about writing it right now. You could make a lot of people – including yourself – very happy and fulfilled in the process. All family historians are in the posterity business – we thrive on what others have left behind. We probably read enough wills to know that you don't really own anything in this life; whatever you have is yours in trust for the duration of this life, and then passes to someone else after you've gone. What will you leave behind for posterity? Will it be a family history that might be read and enjoyed by others for many years to come? I do hope so.

There are several ways of publishing information about your family which others can read and enjoy. You may like the idea of a regular family journal or news-sheet, and you could even issue a full family history in parts over a period of time. In this book we'll assume that you'd like to aim at something rather more substantial – a family history book of one sort or another.

One of the most enthralling aspects of writing a family history is the way in which it's possible to breathe new life back into your ancestors. So a real event which happened in the past – a marriage, for example – might be recorded on a sheet of paper or parchment; from that written record it's possible to re-create the original event in your imagination. Put your imaginative picture into words in a family history, and you've given your ancestors that most precious of gifts, the one that men and women have sought for thousands of years – a touch of immortality. It's worth the effort, believe me!

There are probably as many different approaches to family

A wiredrawer at work. Writing your family history brings events and occupations to life.

history as there are family historians. Some love to collect information and tuck it away like squirrels hoarding nuts; others are only happy when the genealogical programme on the computer is in full swing; others like to spend time quietly contemplating the past and the people who have inhabited it. If you pay a visit to the library of the Society of Genealogists, indulge in a spot of people-watching. Most varieties of family historian are there – from the frenetic gleaner of information, high on nervous tension and rushing around as much as it's possible to rush in such an environment, to the soporific slow reader who seems to be in danger of falling asleep at any moment.

Collecting information – data, if you prefer – about your family is what I think of as high-octane work. As you turn the pages of a parish register or skim through the wording of a will, the engines are firing on all cylinders. It can be exciting and stimulating – which is why so many family historians come back for more, addicted to the adrenal flow of it all.

By contrast, it looks as if the act of disciplining yourself to write down your findings in an ordered way, as a family narrative, might be far less rewarding – boring, even. Not a bit of it! I'll run the risk of being thought rather prescriptive here, and say that if you have only collected data about your family (ancestor spotting, we may call it) and stored the information away safely somewhere, you've only done half a job – or less. The ideal and complete process in my view is this: to *collect* data; to *analyse* it (that is, to make sense of it all) and finally to *synthesise* it (that is, to put it all together so that it has some overall meaning). If you've followed this process through to the end, then writing a family history would be a natural outcome and should not prove too difficult a task. The fact is that writing your family history is also high-octane work; not only that, but the process of pulling all the threads together into a coherent narrative will lead you on to greater discoveries. There will be new questions to be answered, new avenues to explore; your research programme could benefit enormously.

The trick is, of course, that you have to get started. Why not straight away? Here the excuses will come thick and fast, so let's examine a few:

• *I have no time.*

Is time something you have, or something you make? If you say you have no time to do a particular job, what you're really saying is that other tasks must take priority. Of course they must. It would be foolish in the extreme to abandon all your responsibilities to your immediate family just to closet yourself away for weeks and emerge with a completed family history. What you can do, however, is to salvage a moment here, an hour there, even a day or a week in order to get your project underway. Perhaps you could get up earlier in the morning for a few days and put in an hour or two's work before the rest of the world is up and about? If early morning is a bleary-eyed time for you, try grabbing a short spell or two at some other time.

In any case, you probably already spend a fair bit of time on family history matters? New avenues of investigation open up all the time and are practically infinite as one thing leads to another; why not curtail your research programme for a while, and get your adrenal fix from doing a bit of writing?

• *My research isn't finished yet.*

I can't write a family history yet, you may say, because I haven't done a million and one tasks like checking the bishop's transcripts for Hephzibah Gotobed's burial.

Goodness me, I hope your family history research will *never* be finished! What could be worse? Take heart. No piece of historical writing can ever be complete and definitive for all time, and he'd be a fool that would tell you otherwise. All history is conjecture: what we need is information, not completion; truth, not total neatness – or rather, the truth *so far*. James Joyce's original title for the novel which eventually became *Finnegan's Wake* was simply *Work in Progress* – and that is what your account of your family will be. The best you can do is to present a snapshot in time, an account of what you know so far. You will no doubt discover a vital piece of information concerning your family the day after your book is published, and will probably be tempted to say, "If only I'd waited". Eschew all such temptation. Your research won't come to an end, I hope, just because your book has been written. Maybe you'll even produce a revised edition or a second volume one day?

All this is nothing new; consider the sentiments of Henry Cecil Wyld, editor of *The Place Names of Lancashire* (Constable, 1911), who says in his preface (p. vii):

> *In a work of this kind, to strive after completeness and perfection beyond a certain point is to pursue an alluring mirage which recedes further away as one thinks one has reached it.*

It will always feel like the wrong time to put your ideas into print. Tomorrow your family history will be complete, or so you believe – but tomorrow, so the cliché runs, never comes. If you're the kind of person who only feels comfortable with total neatness, then family history is not for you. The fact is that you will have to learn to live with uncertainties, loose ends, unanswered questions – all very frustrating, but the rules of the game, I'm afraid.

Consider a witness in a court of law. New Testament in hand, he or she promises to tell "The truth, the whole truth, and nothing but the truth". Now it's a lamentable fact that some witnesses follow this sacred oath with a string of lies, but even those who don't act in such a way can never tell the *whole* truth. The carefully selective questions put to them by prosecutor and defence advocate alike would soon preclude such a possibility. The function of a trial in a court of law is not to determine the whole truth – it is to establish whether a defendant is guilty of a particular offence as charged, and there are rules to follow. In other words, the focus of a trial is specific, not general. So let's borrow a legal term here: like an advocate in court, give yourself a brief and work to it. Don't aim at completeness, and don't expect to be able to tell the whole truth. The paradox which underlies all this is as follows: to write a good family history, you have to be a perfectionist but also a realist. Set yourself high standards of accuracy, but be honest about what you can and cannot achieve.

- *I'm no good at writing.*

You don't need to be a Shakespeare or a Milton to write a family history. It may be a long time since you wrote anything of any substance, and they may have done little to boost your confidence when you were at school, but you're almost certain to surprise yourself once you get going. A dictionary could be a great help, but if you want to expand your vocabulary or to find a word that has temporarily escaped you, you can't beat a thesaurus (cheap enough to buy, these days), which groups words of similar meaning together and could be your constant desk-side companion.

Don't be hoodwinked into thinking that some people can just sit down and write flowing English with no effort. A fluent writer, like a concert pianist, may start with a natural talent but will have to supplement it with a great deal of work. Very few people indeed can write well without a lot of effort and hard graft, a truth realised in the 18th century by Alexander Pope:

True ease in writing comes from art, not chance.
(*Essay on Criticism*, 1711. Line 362)

By all means enrol for a course at your local college if you really feel you could do with a boost, or follow a distance learning programme, working from home. Meanwhile I've included a mere smattering of hints for good writing later in this book.

Don't be intimidated – have a go!

- *My typewriter's broken.*

Get it mended? Or, if you like, write your story in longhand and then pay someone to type it up for you. Better still, see if you can afford a decent computer with a word processing package. A word processor will allow you to add text, remove it, reposition it, correct it or modify it at will. You really owe it to yourself to go for this option if you possibly can. The typewriting alternative can be messy by comparison, I'm afraid – you'll probably need to use correcting fluid, correcting paper, scissors, paper and glue. Not to be recommended!

Shoreditch Workhouse admissions, 1826 – it is the 'ordinary' families that are increasingly used to illustrate our national history.

Do aim for a PC or an Apple Mac computer if you possibly can. There is a great variety of word processing software available on the market, much of which you can choose to drive using Windows or MS DOS. I've always found that Word Perfect suits my needs very well, though many of my friends swear by Word for Windows and other programmes. Shop around.

You won't forget to save your computer text on a regular basis, will you? A power cut or a thunderstorm could wipe away a few hours' work if you're not careful, and you'd be well advised to save each day's work onto a "floppy" in case the hard disk decides to die over night.

• *My family story is so very ordinary.*

Good! That's what we need! Most famous people and famous families – and not a few infamous ones, too – have already had their biographers. The world doesn't really need too many more books about the Churchills and the Russells, but you will quite probably be writing the first-ever published account of your more modest family. That would be a real achievement! Historians and demographers are increasingly interested in stories of "ordinary" families which made up the great bulk of the population. In any case, most family stories include a significant smattering of individuals who have been far from ordinary, no matter what their station in life may have been.

• *I don't know which ancestral line to write about.*

Make a choice – but start somewhere. Read on for a few ideas.

Any more excuses? No? Good – let's get started.

PREPARING TO WRITE YOUR FAMILY HISTORY

•••••

COLLECTING YOUR MATERIAL

What kind of material will you collect as a basis for your family history? "Material" may include an unsorted pile of grannie's papers and letters (some too intimate and private ever to use in your story?), a bundle of old photographs, a tobacco jar and a pair of cuff links with engraved inscriptions, even a wedding dress or a folding hat in a box.

Beyond your own family treasures, of course, lies the vast world of public records of one sort and another – a world you'll probably want to visit *after* you've made sense of family heirlooms, if you're lucky enough to have any.

Before you turn to records held in public repositories, you would do well to read one or two of the basic guides to tracing your ancestry published over the last few decades – books by A. J. Willis, G. Hamilton-Edwards, A. Camp and G. Pelling; do consider using older books such as *Origines Genealogicae: or, the sources whence English genealogies may be traced from the conquest to the present time* by Stacey Grimaldi (privately published, 1828), and buy or borrow more recent works such as *Tracing your family tree* by Jean Cole and Michael Armstrong (Equation, 1988), *Family Tree Detective* by Colin Rogers (2nd edition, Manchester University Press, 1986) or *The Family History Book* by Stella Colwell (Phaidon, 1980). One of the best overall guides to family history research (now, alas, out-of-print and hard to come by) is the three-volume *Genealogical Research in England and Wales* by David Gardner and Frank Smith (Bookcraft, Salt Lake City, 1956–1966). Your library or local bookshop should be able to help you locate at least some of these, and several other similar books; it certainly does no harm to read more than one, to get a fuller picture.

Don't forget that there is a very close relationship between family history research and local history research; local historians, when all is said and done, refer to much the same source material as family historians much of the time, though the use they make of their findings has a different emphasis. Look, then, at classic guides for local historians such as *Sources for English Local History* by W.B.Stephens (3rd edition, Phillimore, 1994), *Archives and local history* by F. G.Emmison (2nd edition, Phillimore, 1973), *A companion to local history research* by John Campbell-Kease (A & C Black, 1989) and especially *The Parish Chest* by W. E.Tate (2nd edition, Phillimore, 1983).

The material which finds its way into your family history files will probably be drawn from the following sources. This does not attempt to be a definitive list, but should keep you busy for a while:

- Primary sources.

I hope you'll have at least the rudiments of your own private family archive? There may be notes taken from in-depth interviews with elderly relatives, or tape-recordings of the same. You may have jotted down some family legends and traditions which will need evaluating and sifting for any grain of truth each might contain ("One ancestor was a pirate", "We came over with the Huguenots", "Grandfather had the first motor car down his street"). If you're lucky there might be a family bible, diaries, a photograph album, baptismal certificates, and much else. Or perhaps almost nothing at all?

Publicly-held records, potentially bewildering in their range and depth, include civil registration of births, marriages and deaths; census returns; parish registers; bishops' transcripts; marriage allegations and bonds; non-parochial records; wills, administra-

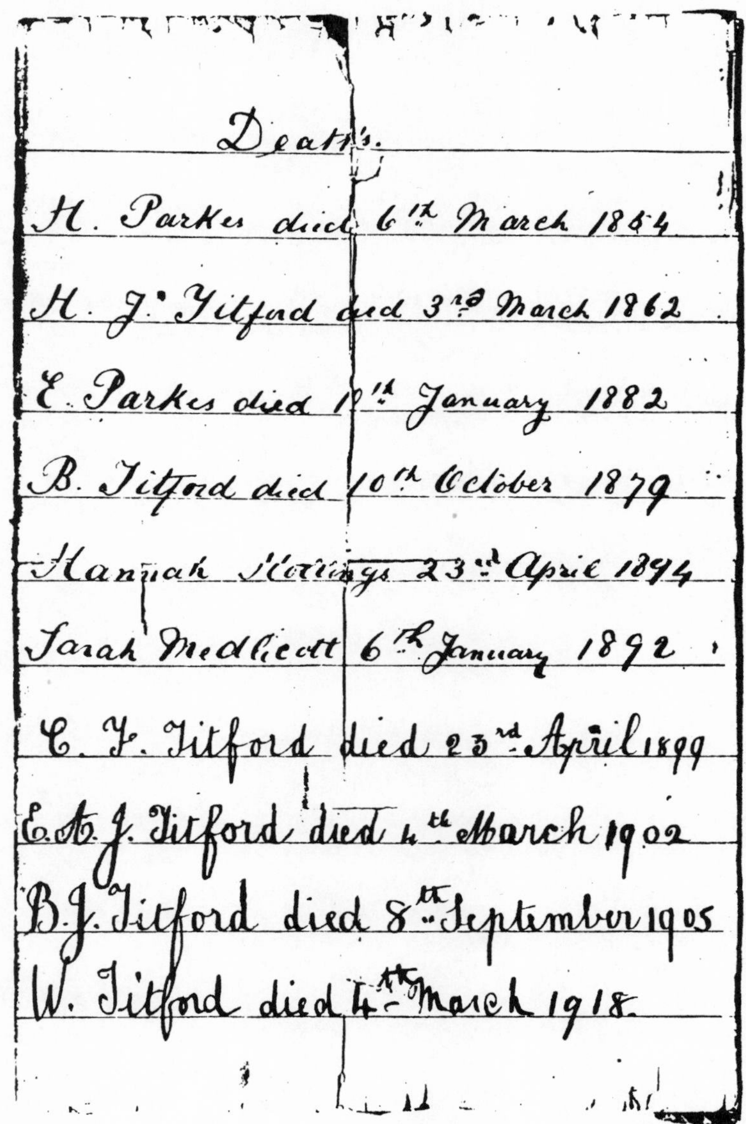

Deaths.

H. Parkes died 6th March 1854

H. J. Titford died 3rd March 1862

E. Parkes died 1[illegible]th January 1882

B. Titford died 10th October 1879

Hannah Hollings 23rd April 1894

Sarah Medlicott 6th January 1892

C. F. Titford died 23rd April 1899

E. A. J. Titford died 4th March 1902

B. J. Titford died 8th September 1905

W. Titford died 4th March 1918.

With luck, family notes will feature in your research files.

tions and other probate records; civil records; parish records; poor law records; diocesan records; quarter sessions records; other legal records; tax records; manorial records; transcripts of monumental inscriptions; newspapers; military records; records of the professions; guild and freedom records; various records of non-conformity; enclosure awards; tithe awards.

And that's just a start! If your research takes you to Scotland, you'll want to examine the Sasine and Service of Heirs records, in Ireland you'll be looking at Griffith's Primary Valuation – and so on. Every country has generated its own original records, many full of names, as a natural part of the administrative bureaucracy which has attempted to keep track of what the population has been up to over the centuries.

- Secondary sources (that is, information copied from, abstracted from, or based upon primary sources).

Books on international, national and local history; biographies, including various editions of *Burke's Peerage* and *Landed Gentry*, *Who's Who* and so on; detailed studies of particular topics (surnames, non-conformity, professions, military, poor law, etc.); commercial directories; telephone directories; poll books; electoral registers; Parliamentary Returns (many being full of names, especially in the 19th century); individual family histories.

Don't forget to look at journals or magazines like *The Genealogists' Magazine*, *Family History*, *Family Tree Magazine*, *Family History News and Digest*, Family History Society journals – and serial publications such as those of local record societies, the British Record Society and the Harleian Society, together with the excellent *Miscellanea Genealogica et Heraldica* and similar publications.

You'll want to consult the International Genealogical Index (the IGI) of the Church of Jesus Christ of Latterday Saints, available on microfiche or CD-ROM. Family History Societies have been in the forefront of publishing a range of useful material for family historians in book form and on microfiche, so look out for their indexes, transcripts and members' interests directories. Jeremy Gibson's guides for genealogists are an

1867.] LONDON ADVERTISEMENTS. 2757

FRENCH POLISHERS, CABINET MAKERS & OILMEN,

ARE SUPPLIED ON THE BEST TERMS BY

JAMES SLIPPER,

87, LEATHER LANE, & 14 & 15, DORRINGTON ST., BROOKE ST., HOLBORN,

WITH SPIRIT VARNISHES, FRENCH POLISHES, SPIRIT LACKERS, &c.,

Manufactured with Spirit of Wine, Duty Free, under the name of Methylated Spirit, as allowed by the Board of Inland Revenue.

	s.	d.		s.	d.	
Superior French Polish	6	6	to	7	0	per gallon
Methylated Finish	4	0	to	5	0	,,
White Hard Varnish	6	6	to	7	0	,,
Brown Hard Varnish	6	6	to	7	0	,,
[illegible] Varnish	9	0	to	10	0	,,

	s.	d.		s.	d.	
Transparent Leather Varnish..	20	0	..			per gallon
Spirit Lackers of all kinds......	10	0	to	12	0	,,
White French Polish	10	0	to	12	0	,,
White Shellac..................	2	6	to	3	0	per lb.

The price is regulated by the Market value of Spirit of Wine.

Gum Arabic, Gum Shellac, Sandrach, Benzoin, and all kinds of Gums, supplied on the Lowest Terms, and a Net Cash List forwarded Free to Purchasers.—Inquiries to be addressed to

JAMES SLIPPER, Wholesale and Export Druggist and Drysalter, French Polish and Spirit Varnish Manufacturer, 87, Leather Lane, and 14 and 15, Dorrington Street, Brooke Street, Holborn.

QUICKSILVER AT THE IMPORTER'S PRICE.

THE BEST WRITING INK.

STEPHENS' BLUE-BLACK WRITING FLUID

Writes a clear, bright, blue colour, and is AS THIN AND AS FLUID AS WATER ITSELF, but changes to an intense black; specially adapted for hot weather and hot climates.

THE BEST COPYING INK.

STEPHENS' BLUE-BLACK COPYING INK.

This article is MUCH MORE FLUID, and DOES NOT THICKEN LIKE THE ORDINARY BLACK COPY INKS. It writes of a clear, full blue colour at first; but both the original and the copies change to a strong black in a short time. Copies may be obtained from it after a MUCH LONGER INTERVAL than with black copying Inks; and the copies are STRONGER and MORE PERMANENT.

Manufactured and Sold by HENRY STEPHENS, Chemist,

18, ST. MARTIN'S-LE-GRAND, LONDON, E.C. (late 54, Stamford Street),

AND BY ALL STATIONERS AND BOOKSELLERS.

TITFORD AND COMPANY,

Furnishing Undertakers,

AND FUNERAL CARRIAGE PROPRIETORS,

231, KINGSLAND ROAD,

6 Doors North of Shoreditch Workhouse;

324, GRAY'S INN ROAD.

Chief Office; 41, JUDD STREET, EUSTON ROAD;

Carriage Department, 45 to 51, ACTON STREET, W.C.

This Company undertakes the entire conduct of Funerals of all Classes at one Fixed Scale of Charges, so that the whole expense may be ascertained and covered by one single payment.

BY APPOINTMENT TO THE GREAT NORTHERN CEMETERY COMPANY.

HENRY SYKES, 67, UPPER THAMES ST., LONDON, E.C.

STEAM ENGINES FROM 4 TO 20-HORSE POWER;

MORTAR MILLS from 5 ft. to 9 ft. in Diameter;

CRANES, HOISTS, CRABS, PUMPS, PULLEY BLOCKS, SAW TABLES, ETC., FOR SALE OR HIRE.

Contractor for Pumping, Sawing, Mortar-Grinding, and other work where Steam Power is required.

Advertisements and entries in commercial directories can be an important secondary source.

excellent secondary source, as is the *Genealogical Research Directory* (the *GRD*) by Keith Johnson and Malcolm Sainty, an international listing of researchers' interests. No serious genealogist's library should be without the genealogical guides by Marshall, Whitmore and Barrow, together with the *Phillimore Atlas and Index of Parish Registers* by Cecil Humphery-Smith (2nd edition, Phillimore, 1995), *The Dictionary of Genealogy* by Terrick Fitzhugh (4th edition, A & C Black, 1994) and *The Local Historian's Encyclopedia* by John Richardson (2nd edition, Historical Publications, 1986). You may also wish to acquire the relevant volumes in Stuart Raymond's ongoing series of county genealogical bibliographies published by the Federation of Family History Societies. Do invest in a microfiche reader if you can, and expect that as time goes by an increasing volume of vital secondary source material will be made available for computer users on CD-ROM.

DECISIONS, DECISIONS . . .

We'd be wise, I think, to work on the assumption that you have more chance of achieving your goal if you know what that goal is before you start. We'll look later at a series of very specific decisions you'll need to make before you start writing, but at the outset there are two questions you must ask yourself before you go any further. These are :

- Which line of ancestry will you follow?

In principle the number of your direct ancestors doubles every generation as you move back. We each have two parents, four grandparents, eight great grandparents and so on. Or do we? If you had nothing but, say, English ancestors (an unlikely possibility, to be sure), then the number of these you would have in the mid-14th century, the time of Chaucer, (doubling up in each generation) would be approximately two million. The population of England at that time was roughly three million people, yet two million of these were your ancestors. It doesn't work, does it? What has happened, of course, is that individuals have married their cousins, near or distant, often without realising the fact. It would only take one first cousin marriage in your family to reduce the number of your ancestors dramatically – suddenly, many of these are "double" ancestors, as it were, and you can't count them twice! There is a process at work here that Cecil Humphery-Smith has called "implection" – rather like implosion, in fact, in that the number of your ancestors doesn't just explode, spraying out more and more the further you go back, but every so often the number falls back upon itself as cousins marry cousins. It's been calculated that individuals of English descent are at most thirtieth cousins of all other individuals of English descent – and many of the people you meet every day will be more closely related to you than that, whether you know it or not.

What does this have to do with writing a family history? Well, you can be brave if you like – foolhardy, some would say – and attempt to write a story that encompasses all your known ancestors on every male and female line. What a pickle you could get yourself into! Better by far to stick to one ancestral line; you'll probably want to feature a male line which perpetuates the same surname, though wives who marry into the family will form part of the story, and their ancestry can be mentioned either in the main text or in notes or footnotes. The surname you feature needn't be your own surname or maiden name, of course; you could start with your great grandmother's maiden name and follow that surname back as far as it will go. Many a very lively and convincing family history has been written in this way. Indeed, there's nothing to stop you writing a family history based upon your husband's or wife's ancestry or that of your best friend. If your book appears with the title or sub-title *The Pilkington Family* or something similar, its focus will be very apparent to any potential readers. Who knows, distant unknown cousins might read it and contact you – and even buy a copy!

• Will you write a chronological account of the family's history starting at some point in the past, or will you give an account of the way in which you conducted your research, working backwards in time from the present as each generation is discovered?

What intrigues and fascinates most family historians above everything else is the research process itself – the way that layer after layer of generations are peeled off, each one revealing the one beneath. You may well have surmounted what seemed like insuperable difficulties; you may have used lateral thinking, delved into scarcely-used original records or made earth-shattering discoveries by virtue of a lot of hard work or even thanks to a great stroke of luck. You may well feel that an account of your researches, taking the reader with you as you face the challenge of moving backwards and sideways through a steadily-growing pedigree would make much more fascinating reading than a simple narrative account of the family's history. I still think that one of the best models to follow if you wish to write such an account is the book by Don Steel, *Discovering your Family History* (BBC, 1980), written to accompany the excellent series of television programmes which featured Gordon Honeycombe's quest for his ancestry. In similar vein, a lesser-known but still fascinating work which you might find in your local library is: *Family Tree: an Adventure in Genealogy* by Nancie Burns (Faber and Faber, 1962).

If you choose to write a "How I did it" book, you could have a lot of fun. It would be unwise to try to formulate definitive rules governing the exact contents or arrangement of such a book; just try to make it gripping, don't give away too much at once, and provide plenty of illustrations. Some of what follows in this book may be useful and relevant to you, but from now on we will focus more precisely on the other option mentioned, a narrative account of a family's history, the alternative most commonly adopted.

Just before we do that, however, there is at least one other approach which you might choose to adopt once you have your notes in apple-pie order: would you be happier after all in producing a book full of family facts and short biographies, a kind of resource book for researchers, rather than a narrative as such? If you do decide upon this option and if it's well indexed, it could certainly be a boon to others. There's always the possibility that you could combine the narrative and resource book elements, the latter by way of substantial appendices. Look at a number of printed family histories to glean a few ideas.

If you *do* write a narrative account, you'll have to put your brain in reverse, as it were. A story which you researched backwards in time – from the present day, one generation at a time into the past – will then need to be told forwards in time as a narrative, starting with the earliest significant date. If you have traced your ancestors back through the records of general registration, from a person's marriage to his or her birth and so on, it's almost tempting at times to believe that your ancestors lived their lives in this way – married first, born afterwards. Oh, no, they didn't!

One further decision will need to be made at some point: even if you decide that you will write about the Pilkington Family or some such, you will still have to choose between a number of options. Will this be your own branch of the Pilkingtons and none other – or will you have at least something to say about all the groupings of Pilkingtons you can find? You may only come up with an answer to this question as you go along, having thought through the implications of the different approaches. Don't delay the decision too long, for all that.

ORGANISING AND ARRANGING YOUR MATERIAL

If you've been assiduous in collecting material relevant to your chosen family and have been working away at such a project for quite a long while, you will no doubt have arranged your notes in some kind of order. I do hope so! If you haven't been so organised, the task of preparing the ground for writing a family history will take that much longer to complete. What might you have done? Perhaps you have a series of files, or computer files, headed Wills, Census Returns and St Catherine's House Records? If you've discovered a batch of family members in, say, the parish registers of Rushton in Northamptonshire (and these are in print, as it happens), you may have entered all relevant entries under the headings of baptisms, marriages and burials. That's fine for keeping your own records neat and tidy, but you can't sit down and write a family history straight from notes organised in this way. Real life isn't and wasn't like this; a person would be baptised, then married, then buried. He or she might appear in census or other records, and may have left a will. In other words, the chronology of a person's life would hop around, in and out of your carefully classified records.

What you need – and if your own experience proves that this is not the case, congratulations! – is a single chronological listing of events which are relevant to your family. From such a list you can then start your story without much difficulty. Ideally your listing would be made with the use of a computer – a word processing package or a database might suit your needs equally well. If not, you can use index cards or sheets of paper fixed into a loose leaf binder. Paper which has already been used but has one blank side may well be perfectly acceptable for this purpose.

Start with any record you choose – not necessarily the earliest one. The first one to hand could be the marriage of William Good to Agnes Peabody in Kendal, Westmorland, on 23 June 1798. Write or type "1798" at the head of the page, then enter the information. You may want to record simply a brief summary of an event, cross-referencing the entry to the fuller details in your main files. When you come to another event which took place in 1798, enter this on the same page; if not, start a new page. Perhaps you can see why a computer is ideal for this task? Your growing chronological list will not restrict itself to family details alone; enter events of local, national, and even international importance. Note that the family village was affected by an enclosure award, a series of bad harvests or an outbreak of cholera in that year; refer to the death of Oliver Cromwell or the accession of King Charles II; mention the fact that the English were busy losing the American colonies at that time – and so on. You will steadily be creating a genuine chronology of events in which births, marriages, deaths, census returns, wills, and national and international events will be mixed up together – exactly as they happened in the real world to real people.

This might sound like a laborious process to undertake, just when you're keen to start writing your story, but it pays dividends in the long run, believe me. You will have the bare bones of your story mapped out before you start. Not only that, but you may well notice connections which had previously escaped you. You might realise that a very large number of family members were buried in different parts of the country in a certain year; was there a national epidemic? You might realise that a certain lady got married very soon after the death of her widowed father; had she been nursing him through his final illness, feeling free to marry only once he had died? A married couple have children every two years, but then there is a six-year gap during the early years of the 19th century; was the husband away fighting against Napoleon?

So, in summary: organising your material under a series of classified headings is fine for everyday use, but will probably not help you when you come to write a narrative, unless you can hold a very wide range of information in your head at one time. What you will also need is a detailed drop-line pedigree to help you organise your thoughts; most people's minds can grasp the intricacies of a family's relationships much more clearly if it is presented in this visual form.

MORE DECISIONS

I promised that I'd suggest some more decisions that you would be wise to make at the outset. Yes, I know that this delays the moment when you start telling your story, and I'm sorry about that, but nothing could be worse than your discovering half way through the writing of your book that you've approached it in the wrong way, or simply can't complete it in the way that you'd hoped to. Do think seriously about the following decisions which will need to be made sooner rather than later:

- Will you be using a word processor programme, and if so, is it the best one for your purpose?

You may have already decided that you will type your book into the computer, print out the final text on your own or somebody else's printer, and then run off copies using some reprographic process or other. Alternatively, you may have it in mind to hand a disk over to your local friendly printer, and get him to print the book for you. Much software these days is compatible, but a quick telephone call to the printer telling him which word processing programme you will be using might be a good idea.

In the event you might not wish to go to the expense of buying some new software just to be able to produce your book, but do give this matter some thought before you start merrily typing away.

- Who exactly are you writing the family story for?

Who are your intended readers? Members of your family? Other family historians? Historians in general? The world? Do try and be more specific in your answer to this question than simply "the general public". In the days when I was a teacher of communication studies, we used to talk about an "awareness of audience". That is, having decided upon your intended readership or audience, keep that audience constantly in mind as you write. Any piece of communication can only be judged to be good or bad, effective or ineffective, in terms of what it aims to do and who it aims to do it for. Do you aim to inform, educate and entertain? Only one or two of these, or all three? As to audience, if you write for your immediate family, you can relax – even share a few in-jokes with them; if you write for a broader readership, you may choose to be slightly more formal. How much do you assume that your readers already know about the arcane world of family history research? Have they heard of the Hearth Tax, do they understand the importance of Hardwicke's Marriage Act, do they know what a settlement certificate was? If you write a statement like this :"I found great-great grandfather in the B.T.s, living in a peculiar", are your readers to suppose that he was a full-blown alcoholic, shacked up in some kind of commune?

Above all you should try to achieve an *empathy* with your readers – that is, try to feel what it is like for them to read your story when they don't have the knowledge that you have, and – worse – may not share your passionate interest in the whole thing. Assume that they need to be won over, persuaded, by your infectious enthusiasm. Don't bore them to death, don't try to impress them with your erudition – but don't patronise them and assume that they know nothing whatever. And, yes, if in doubt, do tell them all about the Hearth Tax, about Hardwicke and about a settlement certificate; if they already know, they'll

200 Hermitage Road
Finsbury Park
N 4

My dear Nephew

Your Cousin Emily & Myself are very sorry to hear the sad news of the loss of your dear Mother and offer you & your Brothers & Sister our deep sympathy in your bereavement she has been a great sufferer but now she is at rest & away from all pain & sorrow may God give you wisdom & strength to discharge all things right in his sight

God bless you all

Yours affectionately

Uncle Walter

I feel Harold like to go to the Funeral so will be at the House at 2 o/c p.m. on Monday

If writing for your own relatives, family letters can add a personal touch.

feel very pleased with themselves, and if they don't know, they'll be glad of the clarification.

- Will you write as a story teller, or as a historian?

I am grateful to Terrick Fitzhugh's excellent book, *How to write a Family History* (A & C Black, 1988), for drawing to my attention the important distinction between the approaches taken by a "story teller" and a "historian". What is that distinction? The historian, unlike the story teller, is apt to make historical judgements as he goes along – indeed, he would regard it as one of his primary functions to do so. Will you make value judgements as you tell the story of your ancestors? Will you criticise your male ancestors for their treatment of women? Will you castigate your forebears for galloping across the countryside in pursuit of a fox, for eating red meat, for not being concerned about the fate of the rainforests or the world's stock of whales? Will you make it clear that you regard your grandfather as something of a misguided dupe for going off to war in 1914, when it now seems clear that the conflict was little more than a cruel and futile European Civil War that should never have happened, a case of pointless carnage? Someone once said that it's easy to have 20–20 vision in retrospect. We can all make supercilious judgements after the event, with the wisdom of hindsight. What, after all, will our descendants make of us? The past, they say, is a different country – and so it is. Why not spare our ancestors the spotlight of anything approaching Political Correctness and its bedfellow, Righteous Indignation? Perhaps we have to accept that most of our forebears led their lives to the best of their ability, given the constraints of the historical period in which they found themselves? If you'd like my own view, it is this: that it isn't helpful to make retrospective judgements on our ancestors, that we should accompany them on their journey through life, walk with them down the tunnels of their lives, not knowing whether there would be light at the end. Share with them their ignorance as well as their knowledge. They may well not have known or suspected that war was about to break out, that the plague was soon to erupt, that they would lose five children in infancy. Just as you would aim to have empathy with the readers of your book, have empathy with your ancestors.

COMPILING THE STORY

I'll make a distinction here between "compiling" your story and "writing" it. Compiling has everything to do with the organisation of your material, whereas writing can be used to mean the day-by-day thud of fingers on a typewriter or computer keyboard. Write in longhand if you prefer!

- Organising your book into sections or chapters.

If you start writing a family narrative, ploughing on until you've finished and then simply stop, you'll have a very strange piece of work on your hands. Your text needs to be organised and arranged in a logical way, if only for the sake of that potentially-bewildered readership of yours. Think in terms of sections or chapters; what will give each of these a coherence and a focus? You might deal with all the Smiths of Appleby in one section, followed by the Smiths of Whitehaven in another, and finish off with the Smiths of Workington. You might deal with one family group (mother and father and all their children) in one section, no matter where they lived or moved to. You might find one individual so fascinating that you think he deserves a chapter all to himself.

Let's pause for a moment. Before you go any further, consider the following question, which might as easily have been listed as one of the key decisions you need to make: will you write an account of concurrent or consecutive lives? In other words, will you deal with several individuals together as a block (a chapter, or a section), or take them one at a time?

The fact is, of course, that the lives of several individuals in your story will overlap in time. Any given decade, for example, may be lived through by brothers and sisters, their parents, their uncles and aunts, their grandparents, their grand uncles and aunts – even their great grandparents and great grand uncles and aunts. The decision you must make at the outset is this: will you write one chapter featuring, say, a pair of brothers called Fred and George together – or will you write a chapter on Fred, and then a separate chapter on George? On balance I favour the latter. If you tell the story of Fred and George together, that is, concurrently, you'll probably end up leap-frogging your way through the narrative. You may take Fred from birth to marriage, then on to early parenthood in a different town; then you'll find yourself writing something like, "Meanwhile, back at the ranch . . . when we last met George he was a babe in arms . . ." and you'll take George into middle age before picking up Fred again and letting him overtake George. This can get very messy and confusing. The one danger you must face if you tell the story consecutively (Fred, then George) is that you'll probably be covering much of the same period of time, and must avoid repetition. By the way, if you think that the distinction between concurrent and consecutive is rather an academic one, consider the case of any criminal who is sentenced to imprisonment for two separate offences: six months and six months, consecutive, means that he serves twelve months in total; six months and six months, concurrent, means that he only serves six months – anything but an academic distinction!

It might help to mention that when I wrote the story of my own family, I adopted the "consecutive" option, following my own direct line of ancestry and compiling one chapter for each adult male in each generation. Every chapter took the man's name as its title, complete with some distinguishing nickname which I had invented for him wherever necessary – so I had chapters with titles like Charles Frederick, Thomas and Margery, Thomas the Alehousekeeper, Ralph the Pauper, Thomas the Calvinist, Charles the Cheesemonger, and so on. Because I hoped to relate each man's life to a period of history, I also used a sub-title for each chapter: The Civil War, Poverty in the Countryside, The French Threat. You can work on the assumption that at least one brother or sister in each generation will be an interesting or unusual character, or that something interesting or unusual will have happened to him or her – which is almost the same thing. Remember that there is a Chinese curse (a curse, notice, not a blessing) which says: "May you live through interesting times". Do also think about what a person did *not* do, as well as what he or she did. Why did great aunt

To the Worshipful the Chamberlain
of London.

SIR,

I DECLARE upon the Oath I took at the time of my Admission into the Freedom of this City, that Charles Frederick Titford who on or about the 1st day of November 1871 was bound Apprentice to George Lambert for 7 Years, did serve 7 Years

after the manner of an Apprentice, and according to the Covenants in his Indenture: and that within that time the said Charles Frederick Titford did neither marry nor receive Wages to his own use, as I know or believe. Dated the 4th day of June 1879

George Lambert

Witness F. A. Baker
Beadle

An apprenticeship bringing the Freedom of the City could give you a 'peg' on which to hang your chapter.

Agnes never get married? Why didn't grandfather fight in the First World War? Why did your ancestor not emigrate to Canada with both his brothers? Why wasn't great uncle Fred apprenticed to a tailor, when all the other boys were?

It is perhaps worth mentioning here that you need not write your chapters or sections in the order in which they will appear in your finished book. By all means write an 18th century section first, followed by one on the 17th century, then return to the 19th century. Just make sure that you read through the whole book at the end, and iron out any creases. It's a seamless robe you're after.

- Setting your ancestors within a wider context.

Let's hope that your chronological notes give at least some broader context in which to set the lives of your ancestors; this should start you on the road to writing a family history as such, leaving the term genealogy (unfairly, perhaps?) to apply to the compilation of pedigrees and rather narrower biographies of individuals in the style of a *Peerage* or *Landed Gentry*.

Men and women in medieval times believed that they were living in a geocentric universe – that is, one that had the earth at its centre. The earth itself was set within a series of concentric spheres – each one invisible, of course – to which various heavenly bodies were attached. The universe, in other words, had more than a passing resemblance to an onion. This image will help us here, I hope. We could think of each of our ancestors as being like the earth in the geocentric system; around each person existed a system of contexts or environments within which a life had to be led. The individual lived within the context of his or her immediate family; that family operated within the context of an extended family; the extended family may have lived within a street or a lane; the street or lane probably lay within a hamlet, a village, a town, or a city; beyond that would be a county or a region, then a nation, then a continent, then the world as a whole. Every one of these contexts could affect our ancestor's thoughts and beliefs, his emotions, his actions, his choices – or the lack of them. The closer the context, the more powerful would be its influence – so the day-to-day affairs of your immediate family would usually impinge upon you more than would the more remote contexts. Usually, but not always, as grandfather would have found out when he received his call-up papers and was whisked off to some remote battlefield during the First World War.

Use these contexts both to explain the actions of your ancestors, and to give the story of your family some substance. Work on the assumption that no man is an island . . .

It wouldn't be far from the truth to say that many of our ancestors were victims of one sort or another. Most of them were victims of the apprenticeship system, whereby a man would need to spend a specific number of years learning a trade; once learned, the trade might then earn a man his living, but it might prove difficult if not impossible to change his occupation in later years. Most people of modest means were victims of the settlement laws; if you strayed across the country, with or without your family, in search of work or a new home, be sure that the parish officials in your new parish would find you out soon enough. Unless you could fulfil certain criteria laid down by the settlement laws, or produce a settlement certificate, they would send you packing – back to your original parish of settlement by virtue of a removal order.

Victims, then. Our ancestors were also answerable for their actions in ways that we might find intolerable. To begin with, there were the neighbours. Only in Australian soap operas are neighbours quite so pleasant to each other so much of the time. In earlier centuries in England and elsewhere you might find yourself living cheek-by-jowl with some fairly objectionable people, nosey, censorious, interfering – violent, even. There may have been few enough chances to escape the pressure – no car or public transport to take you to the nearest town to visit the shops or entertainment centres, no package holidays. Just the neighbours, day in, day out, year in, year out, snooping, criticising, reporting you to the authorities. Above and beyond the neighbours lay a wide range of such authorities to whom you might be answerable, many of them taking great delight in a spot of legalised snooping and keen to slap miscreants back into line. People were victims, again, then, as they found themselves answerable to the officers of the parish, to the Archdeacon, the

Middlesex, to wit. *To the Churchwardens and Overseers of the Poor of the Parish of St.* Clement Dane's, *in the County of* Middlesex; *and to the Churchwardens and Overseers of the Poor of the* Parish of St. Lukes Old Street in the County of Middlesex

WHEREAS Complaint hath been made unto us, Two of his Majesty's Justices of the Peace in and for the County of *Middlesex* aforesaid (One whereof being of the Quorum) by the Churchwardens and Overseers of the Poor of the said Parish of St. *Clement Dane's*, That Judith Graves Single Woman Aged about Thirty Two Years hath

lately intruded and come into the said Parish of St. *Clement Dane's*, and is likely to become Chargeable to the same: We the said Justices upon Examination of the Premises upon Oath, and other Circumstances, do adjudge the same to be true, and do also adjudge the Place of the last legal Settlement of the said Judith Graves to be in the said Parish of Saint Lukes Old Street in the said County of Middlesex

THESE are therefore in his Majesty's Name to require you the said Churchwardens and Overseers of the Poor of the said Parish of St. *Clement Dane's*, on Sight hereof, to remove and convey the said Judith Graves

from and out of your said Parish of St. *Clement Dane's*, to the said Parish of Saint Lukes Old Street afsd.

and her deliver unto the Churchwardens and Overseers of the Poor there, or to some or one of them, together with this our Order, or a true Copy thereof, who are hereby required to receive and provide for her according to Law. Given under our Hands and Seals this 6th Day of August, 1779

John Cox

A removal order 1779 – many people fell foul of the settlement laws.

Bishop, the manor courts, the hundred courts, quarter sessions – and a whole host of other law courts. Our ancestors' lives – like ours, you may say – were circumscribed, as were the choices they were free to make. Their needs were simple enough – food, clothing, shelter, employment – but they also needed a spot of excitement or variety from time to time.

If you can, then, use the contexts within which your ancestors lived to flesh out the story you tell; consider in what way they were victims, and consider the authorities to which they were answerable. If your ancestors made a geographical move (despite the settlement laws), be it to the next village or even to another country, this will add spice and variety to your story. Did they also make significant social or economic moves, up or down the scale? All grist to your story-telling mill!

Above all, do try to get inside the skins of your ancestors – seek that empathy that allows you to share with them what they felt and thought, to experience with them their joys, frustrations, hopes and aspirations. If your research has been thorough and your pedigree is correct, then these people had at least some influence upon your own genetic make-up. Now is your chance to breathe new life back into them, to give their lives, however humble, a further touch of dignity and meaning. Let's hope that one day your descendants may do as much for you!

It will be obvious to most family history researchers that the further you go back in time, the less you will know about your ancestors. You may have stumbled across a "gateway" ancestral link that takes you back through nobility to royalty, but that would be the exception rather than the rule. If you spring from humble or middling stock, you will probably know precious little about your 16th or 17th century ancestors – even if you have found out their names! The trick here is this: the less you know about an ancestor, the more you feature the background when you tell his or her story. After all, the life of a person settled in a small village in centuries past will be inextricably linked with the history of the village itself. Small communities could be claustrophobic places in which everyone knew everyone else – and in which many villagers would be related by blood. So if you tell the story of the village you will in effect be telling the story of your ancestors. If the foreground grows dim, bring up the background, as it were. Have something to say about the operation of the Elizabethan Poor Laws, about the life of a shoemaker, the tribulations of the English Civil War, the stigma of illegitimacy, the price of food, the weather.

A focused programme of background reading should soon equip you for doing this, and will make you feel more of a "proper" historian. Do remember, though, that even when you know *what* an ancestor did and *when* he did it, your judgement as to *why* he acted in the way he did can form part of the story. A difficult task, of course, seeing that many of us don't know why we act in certain ways even in the present! By all means use some conjecture – but don't allow mere conjecture to stand in your text as fact. Suppose, if you like, that your ancestor supported Oliver Cromwell in the 1650s because he was ideologi-

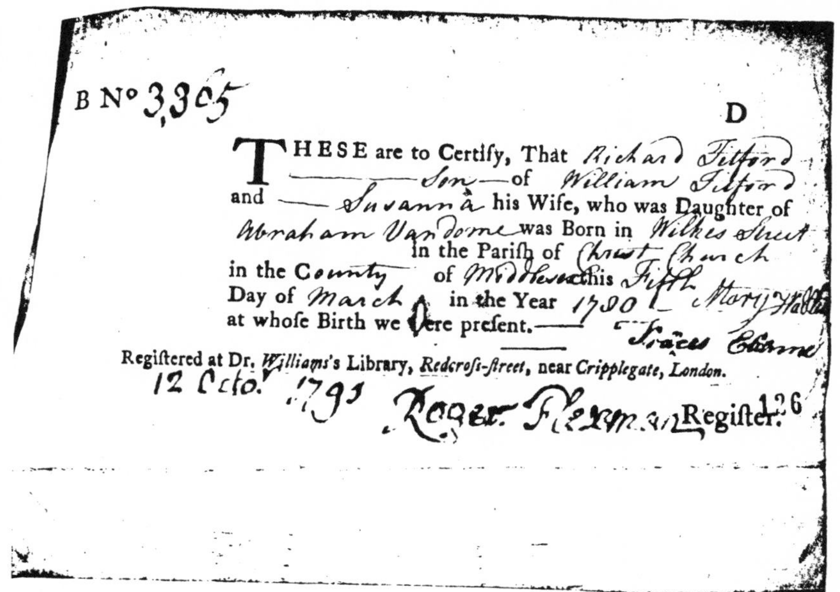
B N° 3305 D

THESE are to Certify, That Richard Fitford Son of William Fitford and Susanna his Wife, who was Daughter of Abraham Vandome was Born in Wilkes Street in the Pariſh of Christ Church in the County of Middlesex this Fifth Day of March in the Year 1790 at whoſe Birth we were preſent.—— Mary Walker Frances Evans

Regiſtered at Dr. Williams's Library, Redcroſs-ſtreet, near Cripplegate, London.
12 Octo.r 1795 Roger Flexman Regiſter. 126

From the Register of Births at Dr Williams's Library. You will need to do background reading to put your ancestors' actions and beliefs in context.

cally committed to the parliamentary cause – but don't state it as a fact unless you have evidence that it is so. Maybe your man would always support the winning side, keen to get on with his everyday business? Suppose, if you will, that great aunt Emily attended the marriage of her cousin Harry even though she would have had to travel many miles to be there – but don't say unequivocally that this was so unless you have definite proof.

As you approach the present day, you may well find that you know too much, not too little, about your ancestors and relations. You won't be able to include everything, and will have to edit. What a good discipline! Not only that, but some of the information you have may well be contradictory. Some people say that great aunt Ada was an adorable, cuddly old lady. Others maintain that she was a real harridan. Which is the truth? Was she one or the other, or a bit of both? It might be foolhardy to attempt a judgement of your own, so why not simply present the alternatives for the reader to think about?

You may have interests of your own, beyond family history as such, which will enable you to bring alive the milieu in which your ancestors lived, giving the reader a real feel for the texture of their everyday lives. You may know something about food in times past, or about music, transport, health or the weather. You may have read a good deal about certain trades or professions; why not reconstruct for the reader a typical day in the life of a blacksmith, a trawlerman, a country doctor or a parson? Costume may fascinate you, and you may be able to say something meaningful about what your ancestors wore, or probably wore. If you know what your ancestors did for a living, look at a book such as *Occupational Costume in England from the 11th Century to 1914* by Phillis Cunnington and Catherine Lucas (A & C Black, 1967). How did your ancestors speak? Would they have used a strong regional dialect or accent? Of all the excellent books on the subject, a recent study by Peter Trudgill, called *The Dialects of England* (Blackwell, 1990), is a scholarly but very readable book.

A study of printed diaries or journals may really bring a period alive for you and could be used directly or indirectly in your narrative. Samuel Pepys and John Evelyn are classics for the 17th century, James Woodforde for the 18th century and

Francis Kilvert for the 19th. Don't forget imaginative literature like novels, which may contain wonderful period detail, especially for the late 18th and 19th centuries. Jane Austen, Charles Dickens, Mrs Gaskell and George Eliot are obvious sources, but so in their way are the Sherlock Holmes short stories and novels. I once taught *Lark Rise to Candleford* by Flora Thompson as part of an A Level English Literature course; it constitutes a wonderful evocation of simple country life in a north Oxfordshire village in the 1880s and 1890s, and I would commend it to you most highly. There are other books you might even find at a car boot sale: *Cider With Rosie* by Laurie Lee, *A Shepherd's Life* by W. H. Hudson, *London Labour and the London Poor* by Henry Mayhew and that wonderful in-depth look at life in a an English village in the early part of the 20th century, *Akenfield* by Ronald Blythe. Plenty to go at here, I hope you'll agree.

Will your own autobiography form part of your story? We will all become part of history one day – if we're not already! – and there is a strong argument for telling your own tale if you feel brave enough. You're hardly going to bare your soul and confess all your misdeeds, are you, but this could be a good chance to share your disappointments as well as your achievements with others. Editing here will be crucial; presumably each of us could ramble on about our own lives for several pages?

Do try to think of all the little details that will give flavour to your narrative. What small, almost insignificant, things were different when you were a child? Did people leave their front door open or unlocked? Was the milk delivered on a horse-drawn dray? Was sugar sold in blue paper bags and toothpaste in flat tins? Did your bag of crisps contain a small twist of blue paper containing salt? Did you need rationing coupons to buy sweets? Was butter patted before you bought it? Did mother make junket? Did father buy Capstan Full Strength cigarettes without tips, or a packet of five Woodbines, or did he have a tin full of shag for his pipe? Did he give you the "fag cards" to flick at school? Did the lady at the shoe shop put your foot in a kind of box with a green light in it to check its size? Did your local drapery store have a system of overhead wires used for conveying an order and cash in little round pots to a central cashier? Did you have a Co-op number for your "Divi"? Did the butcher's boy make his deliveries on a bicycle? Did the coal man wear a fan-tail hat to protect his shoulders and back as he lifted the heavy sacks off the dray, or did you live in a colliery town where the coal was unceremoniously dumped in the street outside each house? Can you still smell that coal dust? Was a copper with a copper stick and a ponch used on wash day – complete with a bag of starch? Did you light the fire with a gas poker? Were there antimacassars on the chair backs? Once father had started the car with the starting handle and was out on the "arterial road", did he salute an AA patrolman on his motorbike who was coming the other way? Did the rag and bone man drift down the street with his horse and cart, shouting some incomprehensible exhortation? Would he really have been pleased if you'd simply offered him rags and bones? Did the blacksmith still work down the street? Were there ceramic inkwells sunk into your school desk? Did you have a snake-shaped fastener on your trouser belt? Did your grandmother call linoleum "oil cloth"? (Mine did!)

Do try jotting down memories like this – you might be surprised how many you come up with. Feature such apparently insignificant details in your autobiography – they will add flavour to what you have to say. After all, your abiding memory of the year 1956, for example, may not be that there was a Suez Crisis going on at home and abroad, but that the milkman fell off his dray one day when he was drunk.

Please can I start writing my story now? I hear you say. Almost now, I reply. First, a word of warning. Whatever you do, don't be too ambitious in what you set out to achieve. Aim to write a succinct story; if it grows as you go along, that's fine, but don't set yourself an impossible task at the beginning. The world is full of unfinished PhD theses. Many a student on a PhD course spends the first year gathering information far and wide, planning a thesis which is totally unrealistic in scope; the second year might then be spent in total despair, and the third in planning an exquisite and suitable suicide. Be warned – keep it manageable from the outset!

So. Your decisions have been made. You have a chronological account of your family's affairs set within a framework of local and national events and a pedigree to work from. You are like a decorator who has carried out the laborious preparation necessary before the real job begins – you've stripped the window-frames of old paint and slapped on a coat of primer. You are now ready to dip your brush into the can of gloss paint – the really creative stage has arrived.

TESTING A SAMPLE

If you don't mind laying yourself open to constructive criticism, you might be brave enough to ask a friend or relation, or both, to give you an opinion of a sample of your book as it develops. Hand over a chapter or a section and ask for an honest opinion. It's unlikely that there'll be anything seriously amiss, but do stress that you'd like a frank comment. You might get a response something like: "Brilliant . . . gripping . . . fascinating – but style rather pompous, can't work out William's relationship to George, a few words I can't understand" and so on. I hope that you'd rather take all this on board sooner rather than later; there may well be minor changes you could make at the outset that could save you a great deal of time and trouble later on.

All right, that being said, you can now start writing in earnest.

WRITING YOUR FAMILY HISTORY

●●●●●

STYLE AND ACCURACY

You're on your own – in more ways than one. You'll probably need to find a quiet place in which you can just sit and be madly creative. But you're on your own in another way – that is, no one can tell you how to write as such. Teachers or helpful friends could give you a few hints regarding good style, could help out in specific matters of grammar, spelling and punctuation, but you will need to write in your own way – ideally in a manner which allows your own personality and view of the world to emerge. Do try to relax, to be yourself. I once had a car which never seemed to want to go into reverse gear; the more I tried to force the gear lever, the worse things became. The only way to persuade the lever into reverse was to make a conscious effort to relax, to stop tensing the muscles. Then it went in like a dream. And so it is with writing: it's possible to try too hard, to strain every brain cell to the point where you can either write nothing at all, or what you do write seems stilted and strained. Try to relax as you write, enjoy yourself, take it easy, use a touch of humour and wit (without being flippant), try to entertain your readers, be bright, enthusiastic.

• Grammar. I was once an English teacher, so I shall give you just a smattering of well-meant advice on matters of good English – but only a smattering, as I don't want you to be intimidated by it all.

You may have noticed that I began a sentence in a previous paragraph with the word "and". Oh, sin of sins! Didn't they tell us at school that "and" is a conjunction, so should never be used at the start of a sentence? What poppycock! That's just one of those dreaded "rules" of good writing that used to keep English teachers in business in days gone by. Rules are made to be broken – once you've understood them and have the confidence to leave them behind.

Pedants will also tell you that you shouldn't split an infinitive. The infinitive (the basic form) of the verb "to go" might look like two words, "to" and "go", but should always be treated as one, with no word squeezed in between the two. The pedants cringe at hearing the famous *Star Trek* phrase, "To boldly go . . .". Sometimes splitting an infinitive can seem ugly or clumsy; on other occasions it seems the only way to convey your meaning precisely without ambiguity. This is another rule to be treated with respect, but broken when necessary. Didn't those same teachers at school tell us that we shouldn't say "Fred and me saw that man"? We were strongly exhorted to say "Fred and I saw that man". Quite right, too. However, a generation of children who had been warned on pain of death never to say "Fred and me" were to grow up using grammatical absurdities like: "That man saw Fred and I". Oh, no, he didn't! That man saw "me", so that man saw "Fred and me". We seem to have ways of half-educating our children! Another old favourite is that rule about never ending a sentence with a preposition – so, to break the rule, "A preposition is a bad word to end a sentence *with*." It does often seem ugly to shunt a preposition to the end, so do avoid it if you can – providing you don't tie yourself in grammatical knots by saying something like, "That is something up with which I will not put".

What about these and similar rules, then? Follow them if you can, but don't get at all paranoid about them, and break any rule if the alternative is to write a piece of ugly and convoluted English. Remember that it was classical scholars, steeped in Latin grammar, who wanted the English language to conform to some of the rules that governed Latin; hence the formulation of a series of rules, many of which are anathema to a living, dynamic language like English.

Having said all that, I do recommend that you try to make appropriate use of the words "fewer" and "less", even if most present-day writers of English do no such thing. If you're speaking about things which are countable – milk bottles, for example – you would have fewer of them. If you're dealing with something in a mass, which isn't countable, like milk, you would have less milk. Now I'm being pedantic!

• Punctuation. Plenty of tripe and nonsense has been written on this subject, too, but don't take it all very seriously. Many a teacher would tell you (and maybe one did tell you once upon a time?) that in an ideal world you would make use of a variety of sentences – short ones and longer complex ones. That's fine if you're happy with it, but my more down-to-earth recommendation would be that you should say what you have to say, finish off your sentence with a full-stop, then start a new sentence. There's no point in ploughing on, building up more and more subordinate clauses and the like, when you could simply bring the whole thing to a halt and start again. I am a great fan of the semi-colon, however, as you may have noticed. Semi-colons are wonderful things – somewhere between a comma and a full-stop, they allow you to hold one statement on ice while you add another one to it. Experiment with them if you like; you probably haven't developed your full potential as a writer unless you've played around with the ubiquitous semi-colon.

Fashions in punctuation have changed over the years; in simple terms, there's now less of it, which might not be a bad thing. So it's perhaps the exception rather than the rule these days to find full-stops used in abbreviations. Your local doctor, who used to be Dr. Smith, M.R.C.S., L.R.C.P., will probably now be MRCS, LRCP without the full stops. Maybe the graphic artists have been influential here, telling us that all those full stops look fussy and ugly? You may have also noticed that a date which would once have appeared as 20th. December has now been shortened to 20 December. Those little endings which used to come after the number ("st", "nd", "rd", "th") are now a threatened species, it seems. Whatever form you use, do be consistent.

You won't forget to use paragraphs, will you? If a sentence

contains one basic idea, expanded or not as the case may be, then a paragraph contains a related set of such ideas. One topic, if you like. The next paragraph you write can boldly begin another topic, or it can open with a linking sentence or phrase to lead you in steadily from the previous paragraph. Vary these approaches if you like.

• Spelling. Generally you've either got this, or you haven't. I have many very intelligent and highly-educated friends whose spelling is abysmal. Or rather, they habitually misspell twenty or so key words. Use a dictionary by all means – though you do need to know at least something about the spelling of a word in order to find it in a dictionary at all! Try to remember that practise spelt with an "s" is a verb, while practice spelt with a "c" is a noun. The same is true of the words license and licence, despite what your local pub or Indian restaurant may think! In the days when mnemonics were offered by teachers to pupils as a way of improving their spelling, my French teacher would point out that there were two "i"s in the spelling of the feminine adjective *vieille*, meaning "old". Substituting "eyes" for "i"s (a dreadful pun), he would then draw a pair of spectacles around the two letters. Corny, but helpful – and you might apply it to that most commonly misspelt of English words, liaise, which also has two "eyes".

If you're using a word processor, you'll no doubt activate the spell-checker. This doesn't solve all problems, of course; some of the terms you'll use in a family history narrative will be unknown to the checker, and if you use the exact wording of an original document or two, the checker will want to "correct" much of it. Unusual words, including names, which you use very frequently can usually be added to the checker's existing memory. Sometimes, of course, the spell-checker will give you some hilarious and way-off-the-mark alternatives; being helpful, it ends up by being ridiculous. Mine offers me artefact (singular) but only artifacts with an "i" as a plural. Very odd. Of course, if I type "twelve pint type" instead of "twelve point type", there will be no correction made, since pint is a perfectly proper word in its own right. A spell checker can perform some very clever functions, but it can't read your mind. I can remember the time when I began writing for *Family Tree Magazine* and was told that there was a spell-checker facility available as part of the Word Perfect software. No need, I thought, I'm quite a good speller. I'd missed the point. A spell-checker allows you to type away, mistakes and all, not correcting as you go along. Then at the end it will do all the checking for you – and it, not you, will carry out the boring task of correcting the spelling. Wonderful things!

• Quotations. You'll probably want to use quotations of one sort or another fairly frequently in a family history. After all, if you've tape-recorded your aunt's reminiscences, why try to re-phrase what she said in your own words? Let her speak for herself! Quote her exact words, indicating those passages you have omitted by the use of three dots in the text. Similarly, quote the exact words used in a newspaper obituary, for example, also editing out inessential sections.

When it comes to including transcriptions of documents written in earlier centuries, however – especially if you're back to the 17th century and before – a problem can arise. Generally the rules of good practice say that you quote the document verbatim, using the original words and spelling, warts and all. I must say that this is what I do myself; unlike some writers, I even transcribe Ye (meaning "the") with a letter "Y", even though I know that the "Y" was just a corruption of an older similar letter-form called a thorn, representing a "th" sound. Spelling from earlier centuries can be a funny thing: if you buy a modern printed text of the works of Geoffrey Chaucer, written in the 14th century, the spelling will usually appear in its original form, but if you look at a printed edition of a Shakespeare play, all the author's spelling oddities and inconsistencies (wild spelt "wilde", "wylde" and so on) will have been ironed out, giving the impression that Shakespeare's writing conformed to modern spelling conventions. Now Terrick Fitzhugh, author of *How to write a Family History*, has a particular view on all this. Horrified by the "Olde Englishe Tea Shoppe" tendency, he takes the view that much original spelling should be modernised, simply to avoid the impression being given that our ancestors were a bunch of quaint buffoons who lived out their lives in a kind of historical theme park. "Life was never quaint," he says, "always real and earnest." You may come across manuscript records in which the words sound outdated and even comical ("Thou naughty varlet" and the like), but at least you can ameliorate matters by modernising the spelling. I take Terrick's point; you must now decide how you wish to proceed.

THE PROCESS OF WRITING

Writing a book, be it large or small, is a funny old business. Talk to some people who have done it, and see what their feelings are.

To begin with, you may find that your creative energy – and you will certainly have some! – comes in fits and starts. Some days you will sit down to write and the words just won't come out in the right way. You can't turn fluency on like a tap, and if you're tired, or your mind is on other things, there'll be days when you creak your way through the writing process. There are two views on all this, and I won't be prescriptive about which you will find most convincing. There are those who say that you should be disciplined in your approach, forcing yourself to sit down and write, say, for an hour each day, for a two-hour slot each week, or whatever. Others will maintain that there is little point in hitting your head against a brick wall if the words just won't come; leave it for a while, wait until the creative muse is on top form, and sit down for a writing session whenever you feel the urge, sticking at it for as long as you can.

Whichever of these strategies you adopt, you really do need to be disciplined to some degree if you are ever to finish your task. Set yourself an overall deadline ("I will have finished this family history a year from now") and, if you can, short-term deadlines as well ("I will have written three chapters by the end of next month"). Deadlines – and they should be realistic deadlines – focus the mind wonderfully; they will sometimes force you to keep going even when you don't much feel like it (not always a bad thing) and they will probably persuade you that you'll simply have to leave some things out of your story – that is, to edit. Also no bad thing! Some people work well under pressure, others don't, but you must put at least some pressure on yourself if you are to write your family history. If you don't, then Parkinson's Law will operate, your time will be filled up with other things, and you'll get nowhere. There will always be some task or other which you will have to lay aside if you are to do some serious writing. The ironing may have to wait, the weeds in the garden may have to be ignored for a while, your pile of correspondence may have to remain unanswered, you may have to leave your car unwashed this week (or this month?). If you allow everyday life to crowd out your writing time, then rest assured that it will do just that. You may even find that the time you spend being creative as a writer puts a certain amount of strain upon your relationship with your own family – which is why a number of books carry a dedication to the author's husband, wife and/or children "for their patience and understanding while this book was being written". It's really a matter of balance, isn't it? No point in breaking your own present-day family asunder just to write a story of what your family got up to in the past!

So, I repeat, writing a book is a funny old business. You may even find that male authors will tell you that bringing their book to completion is the nearest thing a man can ever get to having a baby! Indeed, there are similarities – especially when, after months of patient work, it seems at times as if the book will never be finished, the birth will never happen. At least once your book is written, you can sit back and relax for a while – you won't have to feed it, change its nappies or be kept awake at night by its crying! To me, one of the most aggravating things about writing a book occurs at the stage when you really do think that you've almost finished, that only a few things remain to be done. Just the introduction to write, the bibliography to compile, the illustrations to be chosen and captioned, the final proof-reading to be done, and so on. Maybe by that stage you've exhausted yourself or allowed your creative energy to run low, but the last steps in the process of bringing a book to completion are always the most frustrating to me. Don't let me put you off; it may not be like that for you!

One other thing will probably happen to you: your subconscious mind will be churning away a lot of the time, thinking about what you've already written and what you intend to write next. Flashes of inspiration may come to you when you're driving the car, digging the garden, hanging out the washing, listening to a sermon or watching television. Don't let such flashes sink down again into the nether regions; jot down a few notes on a piece of paper for future use – or use a small hand-held tape recorder (in a car, yes; during a sermon, no). If the bug really bites you, you might even wake up in the middle of the night and find yourself, bleary-eyed, scrawling a note or two in case you've forgotten it by morning.

EDITING AND REVISION

You'll be editing in two different ways as you proceed. To begin with, there's the family history material which will form the basis of your book, some of which you'll decide to use and some of which you'll have to reject, no matter how reluctantly. In other words, you'll need to edit in some things and edit out others. Don't include everything you know about your family just because you know it; if you do, you'll clog up your text and neither you nor the reader will be able to see the wood for the trees. Your accumulated family information is a source *from which* you will write your narrative; you'll have to be selective. Don't include material which is unduly tedious, repetitive or only peripheral to the main thrust of the story.

You may want to think very carefully about whether you'll let skeletons out of their cupboards. You may feel that they should be let out, shaken, dusted down and included – if only because you're writing a family history, not building a family monument. It won't always be so simple, alas. You might think that unearthing a bit of scandal – illegitimacy or minor crime – is all part of life's rich tapestry, but there may be those still alive who had carefully kept the skeleton cupboard door closed and who would be quite genuinely (if unjustifiably?) upset if you were to include material which they regard as embarrassing or even shameful. You do want to tell the truth, but you don't want to cause offence. If you can, talk it all through with anyone who might be worried, to see if you can come to some compromise. If not, try to gauge the depth of feeling you're encountering and act accordingly. Is it worth causing deep offence to a close relation for the sake of writing a book that pulls no punches?

So you'll need to edit your raw material, deciding what goes in and what stays out. Not only that, but once you've started writing you'll also need to edit or revise your text. If you were a genius beyond measure, you'd simply sit down, write a book from start to finish, stop, and publish. Alas, for us lesser mortals life isn't quite like that. You really will have to go in for editing and revision of some sort – not root and branch, we hope, but significant for all that. My own favoured way of proceeding is as follows: I write a certain amount of text – a chapter or a section, possibly – and I then leave it for a few days at least, maybe longer. Then I return to it and make revisions as necessary. I'll correct spelling or punctuation errors, I'll re-phrase sentences that sound clumsy or where the meaning isn't clear. I may cut out whole paragraphs or even pages because I don't think they're necessary any more, and I may rearrange other blocks of text. You can see why a word processor is so vital if you want to do this job swiftly and efficiently! There was a time when I would have used off-cuts of paper and a pot of glue. Perish the thought!

I'm sorry to say it, but you really can't afford to be too precious about certain passages you've written. Even if you sweated blood to complete a page or two of text, you must be brutal at the revision stage if you decide that it isn't so vital or interesting after all. The more you prune your text, the stronger it will be. To change the metaphor: I always say that it's easier to cut dead flesh than living flesh. The moment after you've finished writing a page or two, nothing would persuade you to abandon it or to edit it severely. Two weeks later you can perhaps take a more detached view. Yes, you thought it was good at the time, it cost you a great deal of energy to write it, it was once precious to you – but now it must be brutally cut. The writer's waste-paper basket, like the film editor's cutting room floor, will eventually be full of wonderful material that somehow failed to make it into the final version.

You will be writing your book in sections over a period of time. You might not even compose the chapters in the final order in which they will appear, and your style or your sense of humour may change over weeks and months. At some stage you'll have to weld all the pieces of your book together. Having edited each section to your satisfaction, you'll now have to sit down and read the whole thing through from start to finish. Are there inconsistencies? Have you repeated yourself? Has your writing style or your level of humour changed? To repeat, you're aiming at a seamless robe; the reader should not be conscious of fits and starts in your final book. Or, another metaphor, be like a French polisher – smooth and polish your work until it shines. Once your story is finished it may well be longer than you'd planned that it should be. Are you happy with that? It very often happens, and you may not want to cut it down significantly in size.

What about proof-reading? The first time I ever wrote a book, I asked a friend who had once worked for a printing firm to proof-read the final manuscript. After all, he'd had experience, hadn't he? I know now why my friend only agreed to this request rather reluctantly. There is really no magic about proof-reading – it's just a laborious and time-consuming task.

You will almost certainly need to read through your final work more than once: checking for factual accuracy is one thing; making sure that the text is clear and unambiguous is another; ensuring that your small numbers in the text refer to the appropriate note at the back or wherever is another; looking for "typos" – that is, mechanical errors of typing – is another. If you feel confident enough, try to look for all these features at once – but be warned, it isn't easy. Your brain prefers to have its tasks separated, not all lumped together. If you're reading through looking for "typos", don't for goodness' sake get too *interested* in what you're reading. That's fatal! You'll rush ahead to get to the next page, and your eye won't see, or your brain won't register, some glaring errors. There is even a rumour around that some professional proof-readers tackle a book from back to front, so that the sense doesn't get mixed up with the typographical accuracy!

Proof-reading, then, is not the same as simply reading. You should try to be detached, objective; read in a staccato way, letting your eye take in every word separately. Keep your reading jerky – try not to let your eyes flow along ahead of your brain. Often it's the big things that escape your notice, not the small ones. Ask anyone who proof-reads *Family Tree Magazine*, for example. If the team of proof-readers misses anything at all, it'll probably be some huge bold title, set in large-point type, not a small detail in the main text. A final thought: no matter how many times you read your text through, no matter how careful you are, no matter how many people do the job (and it's a fact that different people spot different mistakes), the strong likelihood is that there will still be a few errors in the text on the day you publish. You'll probably spot these on the very next day – that's the unfairness of it all.

AN EXAMPLE OF FAMILY HISTORY WRITING

As we are now approaching the end of this section on the writing of a narrative, you might think it unfair of me if I were simply to offer you well-meant advice without giving you a brief example of my own work in this regard. A short passage from my book *The Titford Family 1547–1947* (Phillimore, 1989) follows. This is not intended to be a classic example of good writing or anything of the kind; rather, I think you might find it interesting to consider the various sources I used in order to compile this single sentence. Let me sketch the background very simply. In the year 1798 the worthy people of Frome in Somerset established a home-based fighting force called the Frome Selwood Volunteers formed – in theory, at least – to help repulse an anticipated invasion by Napoleon and his troops. My namesake John Titford, second son of Charles Titford, cheese-monger and pig butcher, joined up as an infantryman. He may have been a brave volunteer, but he was not a healthy man, and on 2 February 1799 he died of consumption at the age of twenty-four and was buried with full military honours. My story continues like this:

> *It can have been no easy journey for the funeral procession of mourners and military volunteers as they followed the coffin up the steep climb to Catherine Hill Burial Ground that bleak Friday in February with the snow thick on the ground.* (p. 98).

The question is this: where did the information contained in this sentence come from? Let's take a few words at a time:

• "No easy journey". The journey ended at the burial ground and would have started from the family home. Where was that? How do we know? The Titfords lived at the first house on the east side of Pig Street, Frome, near the bridge. Notice that in days when a street worked for its living its name was an uncompromising Pig Street, not Acacia Avenue or some such pretentious alternative. The detailed Frome rate books for the latter years of the 18th century establish this address for the family, information which is reinforced, as it happens, by a contemporary turnpike deed and by records of the Frome Literary Institute which was eventually built on the site of the family house.

• "Mourners and military volunteers". How do we know that this was a military funeral? The family were practising Baptists throughout much of the 18th century, and are significantly absent from the baptismal and burial records of the parish church of St John – a bleak enough scenario for any family historian. However, the burial registers for Badcox Lane Baptist Chapel in the town do exist for this period, and may be consulted at the Public Record Office in London. The Badcox Lane minister, John Kingdon, gave the kind of extra detail in his burial register that may not have appeared had this been recorded by the local vicar: "John Titford. Aged 24. With Military Honours". A list of volunteer infantrymen which appears in a printed history of the Frome Volunteers duly includes the name of "John Tizford" (sic). Not only that, but across the road from the Titford home lay the Frome Bluecoat School, and the son of the master there, Edmund Crocker, kept a diary during this period which has survived the ravages of time. His diary entry for 2 February reads:

On the 2d instant died in a consumption J Titford aged about 4 or 5 & 20 years. He being a volunteer in our infantry, he was this day interred with the military honours due to him.

I John Boys do voluntarily Inlist myself as a private Soldier, to serve his Majesty King GEORGE, in the Regiment of Foot commanded by the hon^ble Col^o John Batereau and in Capt James Gages Company, as Witness my Hand this 27 Day of Septr in the Year of our Lord, 1742.

John Boys

THESE are to certify, That John Boys of Leeds in ye County of York by trade a Cloath Drosser came before Me, One of his Majesty's Justices of the Peace for the said County, and acknowledged to have voluntarily inlisted himself to serve his Majesty King GEORGE, in the abovesaid Regiment and Company. He also acknowledged he had heard the Seventh and Tenth Articles of War Read unto him against Mutiny and Desertion, and to have received his Majesty's Bounty Money, and took the Oath of Fidelity, according to the Direction of the Twenty first Article contained in the said Articles of War, viz. Rules and Articles for the better Government of his Majesty's Horse and Foot Guards, and all other his Land Forces in the Kingdoms of Great-Britain and Ireland, and Dominions beyond the Seas; and took the Oath following.

I John Boys - - - Swear to be true to our Sovereign Lord King GEORGE, and to serve him honestly and faithfully in Defence of his Person, Crown and Dignity, against all his Enemies and Opposers whatsoever. And to observe and obey his Majesty's Orders, and the Orders of the Generals and Officers set over me by his Majesty. So help me GOD.

Sworn the 27 Day of Septr in the Year of our Lord, 1742 Before

John Snowden mayor

I Do hereby certify, That John Boys made Oath before me, and in the Presence of Thos Crosler Corple of the above-mentioned Regiment, that to the best of his Knowledge and Belief he was born in Great-Britain, in the Parish of Leeds

and that he is sound in Body and Limbs.

the Day and Date above-mentioned.

Sworn before Me

John Snowden
mayor

An Enlistment Certificate of 1742, evidence of a military career.

• "The steep climb to Catherine Hill Burial Ground". How do we know that the climb was steep? Easy: visit the town, locate the old site of the burial ground and walk it for yourself!

• "That bleak Friday". How do we know that 2 February 1799 was a Friday? It's simply a matter of using a perpetual calendar of some sort; in this case I referred to that excellent publication, *Handbook of Dates for Students of English History* by C. R. Cheney (corrected edition, Royal Historical Society, 1978).

• "With the snow thick on the ground". How do we know there was snow? Local newspapers contain accounts of the appalling conditions prevailing at this time, with Frome suffering its heaviest fall of snow since 1767, and over in Norfolk, Parson Woodforde, the diarist, was writing that such severe weather had not been known for the last sixty years.

I hope you'll feel that this has been a useful example of how much information – information that may take weeks or months to unearth – can be packed into just a few words. This is what I meant when I referred earlier to the act of synthesising your family history data into a narrative which is based upon fact but which will hopefully help the reader create a scene in his or her own mind. I've tried here to bring the past alive – or to bring it alive *again*, if you prefer.

I sometimes think that writing fiction would be easy; much of the time you'd be in control of the facts. Writing history or family history is different: the facts must be in control of you.

PREPARING TO PUBLISH YOUR FAMILY HISTORY

●●●●●

Now you've written your family story, the core of your book. You're fast approaching the publication stage, but there'll be a few added extras to think about first. Let's start by offering you a detailed list, complete with some explanatory comments, of what your finished book could contain. I say could, because not every publication will contain every single element mentioned here. Common sense should tell you that your book may not carry a dedication, but that it should have a title page – and so on.

THE ELEMENTS OF A BOOK

We'll move from the front of a book to the back.

- A title.

You may have had a title in mind for your book right from the outset, or you may have finished all the writing and still be praying that inspiration will come. A title may come to you in a blinding flash, or you may need to sit down and carefully consider the options. Why not ask a few friends and family members what they think? You can always turn down their suggestions politely if you need to.

When I wrote my book on the Titford family, I originally entitled it *Come wind, come weather*, but when it was eventually published, it had become simply *The Titford Family, 1547–1947.* I had some reservations at the time, but I knew that the publishers were keen that this book should sit alongside the many other publications they had on their lists with similar titles. In fact I think that neither title is ideal; *Come wind, come weather* has a nice Bunyanesque ring to it, but tells you little enough about the content, while *The Titford Family* is rather bland, and suggests that the book covers all branches of the family, which it never intended to do.

I wish you many happy hours of thinking up a title. Here are a few invented examples, from the plain to the more ornate, to get you pondering:

The Fortescues; Fortescue Records; The Fortescue Family; The History of the Fortescue Family; The Fortescue Story; My Fortescues; The Fortescue Papers; The Fortescues of Essex; Fortescue and Related Families; Three Generations of Fortescues; Fortescues – London Goldsmiths; The Fighting Fortescues; Forte scutum salus ducum: the Fortescues of Devon; Born to rule [the name of Fortescue not mentioned]; *A Devon Family* [the name of Fortescue not mentioned].

- Front cover/dustjacket.

If your book is softback (that is, with covers made of paper, card, linen-effect card, laminated card or whatever), you will have a front cover to play with. Alternatively, you might have a hardback book with no dustjacket – or one with a dustjacket.

In each case, you'll have a front and back cover (softback or hardback) or a front and back of a dustjacket at your disposal. If a hardback book has a dustjacket, then the boards themselves (usually covered with cloth or simulated cloth) are usually plain.

Your title and the author's name will normally adorn the front cover/front of dustjacket, so that's a start. What else might you feature? A reproduction of a photograph, a drawing, a map? Do provide a caption for such an illustration on the dustjacket flap or at an appropriate place inside the book. For an impressive result you could superimpose the title and author's name on any illustration you use. On the other hand, you might decide to go for a very plain cover with minimal use of colour. If you do use a photograph, you could run it right to the very edges of the dustjacket or front board, a device known as "bleeding off the edge".

Producing an attractive and eye-catching cover could be an expensive business if you want a full range of colours. You might feel that it's worth the expense: they say you can't judge a book by its cover, but many a book has sold itself to a series of potential readers because it simply looks so nice as they pick it up.

The inside cover of a softback book is very often left blank, but it might contain a brief summary of the book's contents to give the reader a flavour of what is to come. The inside flap of a dustjacket is very often used for this purpose.

Then there's the spine – if the book is thick enough to have one. This will feature the book title and the author's name; a dustjacket, if there is one, will repeat this information. If you've produced a fat and chunky book, you might be able to fit the words across the spine horizontally; if not, the reader will have to turn his head to one side to read the information as it runs up or down the spine. I say "up or down", because there really is no consensus as to whether a title should read up the spine from the bottom, or down the spine from the top. I've spent so many years collecting the publications of the Harleian Society that I've grown accustomed to the "up from the bottom" style. Many modern books use the reverse method – but some don't, so you have a choice. In theory you might be able to fit the author's name across the top of the spine horizontally, leaving the title to run up or down beneath it. Anything that looks good is acceptable.

- Preliminary pages ("prelims").

Bibliographers refer to the first few pages of a book, those that come before the main text, as the "prelims". Pages which come between the title page and the main text (that is, the contents page, foreword, etc) are sometimes un-numbered, but could begin at number 1, continuing on uninterrupted once the main text begins. A more classical – classy, I would say – way of doing this is to number every page between the title and the main text with lower-case Roman numerals: i, ii, iii, iv, v, and so on. Look at one or two books, old and new, to see exactly what each one does in this regard.

- Endpapers.

Open a case-bound (that is, hardback) book at the front. You'll notice that one piece of paper, twice the width of the book, has been folded vertically down the centre, one half being stuck to the front board, the other half standing free as the first "page" of the book itself. These constitute the front "endpapers". The stuck-down half is referred to as the "front pastedown", while the loose half is known as the "front free endpaper". It should come as no surprise to learn, therefore, that such a book will also have a rear pastedown and a rear free endpaper. Normally endpapers are left blank, but you could use them to feature an illustration or a map. A book with paper or card covers will not have endpapers as such, though it may have a plain page bound in at the beginning and another at the end.

- Half-title page, or simply "half title".

This is a sheet which simply carries the title of the book, and usually nothing else. A great favourite in times gone by, it is rather less commonly found now than it used to be.

- Title page.

Here you'll find the title (in large print) and any sub-title in smaller print. There will also be the name of the author (or editor), and of any collaborators whose contribution to the finished work has been of significant value. At the foot of the title page the publisher will place his name, and often his logo if he has one. The year of publication also sometimes appears on the title page.

Over the years I have written many book reviews of privately-published family histories, and I must confess that I give those without a title page a hard time. Why spoil the ship for a ha'p'orth of tar? A book with no title page seems as incomplete as would a menu in a good quality restaurant that offered no starters, only the main course. Sometimes I come across family histories – and other published books and booklets on family history topics – which omit a title page and start the text on the first available left-hand page – even on the inside cover! It's easy to see why this should be so; in a way every page is vital, and we don't like leaving blank spaces. In my mind this is false economy.

Please, give your readers space in which to breathe! A good book, like a good meal, should be approached gently and steadily, gaining substance as it goes along.

If you were feeling really ambitious, you could even superimpose the words on your title page onto a faint background picture – an engraving or a drawing. Now we're getting very sophisticated!

• Reverse of the title page.

This is reserved for a range of factual information of a bibliographical kind which you should aim to provide:

o The name and address of the publisher.
o The date of publication of this and any earlier editions.
o Copyright symbol (a letter "C" placed in a circle), together with the name of the person holding the copyright (usually the author).
o An International Standard Book Number (ISBN).
o Cataloguing-in-publication details (CIP).

A certain amount of mystique surrounds these last three features, but each is easy enough to arrange. The British Library and the Standard Book Numbering Agency have joined forces. In advance of the publication of your book (allow three months or so) write to The Standard Book Numbering Agency at 12 Dyott Street, London WC1A 1DF (telephone number: 0171 836 8911) and ask for an International Standard Book Number and a form to complete for cataloguing-in-publication. One advantage of doing this is that your book will then appear in bibliographies such as Whitaker's *Books in Print*, which many booksellers now use in microfiche or CD-ROM format. To get an ISBN, you will need to provide the name of the publisher, a postal address, a telephone number (and FAX number if there is one), a name of a contact, a VAT number if relevant, and a photocopy of the text you will use for your title page and rear-of-title or "imprint" page. An ISBN will cost you nothing and it will act as a unique reference to distinguish your book from all others. Place it on the rear of your title page and on the back cover. When I wrote and published a series of books on Derbyshire dialect with a friend called Richard Scollins under the title *Ey Up Mi Duck!* in the late 1970s, the first volume had the ISBN: 0 9505292 0 6. Here the first "O" identifies Britain, "9505292" is the number allocated to us as publishers, and "0 6" specifies the particular book.

As to establishing your copyright, when the book is finally printed you should send a copy to the Legal Deposit Office, British Library, Boston Spa, Wetherby, West Yorkshire LS23 7BY. In the course of time, agents acting on behalf of five other British Copyright Libraries (including the University Libraries of Oxford and Cambridge) will write to request that you send them a free copy, too. You should comply willingly with this request. At least you can have the satisfaction of knowing that a copy of your book will be safely lodged in a number of libraries long after you've shuffled off this mortal coil.

If you really want to scare off any plagiarists who might use parts of your book without permission, you could add a stern warning on the back of your title page saying something like this:

> *All rights reserved. No part of this publication may be reproduced, stored in a retrieval system or transmitted in any form or by any means, electronic, mechanical, photocopying, recording or otherwise, without the prior permission in writing of the publisher.*

Your copyright as author of your book is yours until you die (unless you choose to sell it or rent it to someone else), at which time it passes into your estate and persists for at least fifty years thereafter.

British Library Cataloguing-in-Publication Data. When you write to the Standard Book Numbering Agency, you can request that they provide you with a bibliographic reference to appear on the rear of your title page. At least three months' notice must be given. A typical example would look like this:

Fitzhugh, Terrick V.H.
How to write a family history.
1. Great Britain. Genealogies. Compilation
& publishing – Amateur's manuals.
I. Title
808'.066029021

The printer's name and address, if relevant, often comes below everything else at the foot of this rear-of-title page.

- Dedication page.

Frequently this will consist of just a few words, generously spaced, almost lost on an otherwise empty page. A dedication is no more essential to your book than is a key-note quotation (see below), but you may feel that it provides a unique opportunity for you to thank or to show great esteem for a person or group of people. You may consider it appropriate to dedicate a book on family history to your parents or grandparents, your husband, wife, children or grandchildren, rather than to your dog or your parrot. Whoever you decide upon, that person will probably be extremely grateful to you – even touched or moved by your gesture. You may want to add a short phrase after the person's name, something like: "To Susan, who knows how much she has helped to make this book possible". You may even make a dedication to your family at its broadest: "To an exceeding great army of Champneys" or "To all Carringtons far and wide". Be guided by good taste and by the desire to make someone feel happy and even flattered. Many books from previous centuries contain excruciating grovelling and flattering dedications to the rich and famous (or to some person who forked up the cash for the book to be printed) which you probably won't want to emulate.

• Reverse of the dedication page.

This can either be left blank, or used for some appropriate purpose such as an appeal from the author to the readers to provide more information on the family in question if they possibly can. Alternatively, you could use the reverse of the dedication page for a "key-note quotation".

• Key-note quotation.

I'm using this term to refer to a literary quotation of family history significance which a writer might use as the opening statement in his or her book. If you use one, preferably let it be one that means something to you, or is borne out by the book you have written.

My own family history book opened with that over-worked (though terribly appropriate) quotation from Sir Arthur Conan Doyle's *The Sign of Four*:

> *When you have eliminated the impossible, whatever remains, however improbable, must be the truth.*

Perhaps you can find a rather less clichéd example to get you started? Here are a few taken from the opening page of a book called *Memorials of an ancient house – Lister/Lyster* by Rev. H. L. Lyster Denny (1913):

> *Look unto the rock whence you are hewn, and to the hole of the pit whence ye are digged.* (Isaiah li,1).
> *Let us now praise famous men and our fathers that begat us.* (Ecclesiasticus xliv,1)
> *People don't know how entertaining a study it [genealogy] is – who begat whom is a most amusing kind of hunting; one recovers a grandfather instead of breaking one's neck – and then one grows pious to the memory of a thousand persons one never heard of before.* (Horace Walpole)
> *No people will look forward to posterity who do not often look backward to their ancestors.* (Edmund Burke)
> *He who takes no pride in the noble achievements of remote*

ancestors will never achieve anything worthy to be remembered with pride by remote descendants. (Macaulay)
Ev'n the homely farm can teach us
There is something in descent (Tennyson)
Rely upon it, the man who does not worthily estimate his own dead forefathers, will himself do very little honour or credit to his country. (W. E. Gladstone)

You may find some of these a trifle pompous (sexist, certainly!) but if you keep your eyes open, you may find something a little more down-to-earth. The use of an opening quotation isn't compulsory, but it's nice if you can find one that really means something to you.

- Contents page.

List your chapters or sections, using one line for each, giving the page upon which each begins. If your book has not been arranged along logical lines, this should become immediately apparent from scanning your list of contents. Let's hope you don't have to confront this problem at such a late stage!

- List of illustrations.

You may also wish to make a list of your illustrations, giving relevant page numbers. You could itemise your pedigrees separately if you wish.

- Foreword.

Certainly not compulsory. A foreword is usually written by someone other than the author. Some dignitary or other may be prepared to endorse your book and sign his or her name at the bottom. The wording of the foreword may even be composed by you or by the publisher, requesting the busy dignitary simply to sign in agreement, yes or no!

- Preface.

Also not compulsory. A preface could provide an opportunity for you to make some general statements about your book, your

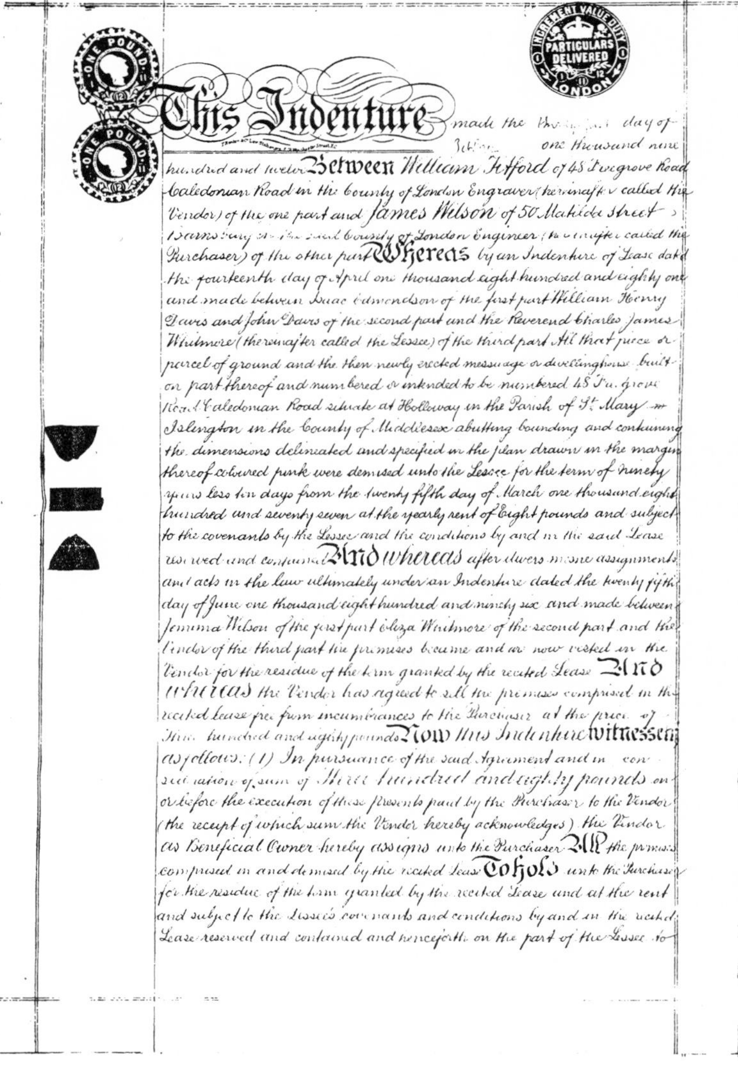

This Indenture made the [illegible] day of [illegible] one thousand nine hundred and twelve **Between** William Fifford of 48 Ivegrove Road Caledonian Road in the County of London Engraver (hereinafter called the Vendor) of the one part and James Wilson of 50 Matilda Street Barnsbury in the said County of London Engineer (hereinafter called the Purchaser) of the other part **Whereas** by an Indenture of Lease dated the fourteenth day of April one thousand eight hundred and eighty one and made between Isaac Edmondson of the first part William Henry Davis and John Davis of the second part and the Reverend Charles James Whitmore (thereinafter called the Lessee) of the third part All that piece or parcel of ground and the then newly erected messuage or dwellinghouse built on part thereof and numbered or intended to be numbered 48 Ivegrove Road Caledonian Road situate at Holloway in the Parish of St. Mary Islington in the County of Middlesex abutting bounding and containing the dimensions delineated and specified in the plan drawn in the margin thereof coloured pink were demised unto the Lessee for the term of ninety years less ten days from the twenty fifth day of March one thousand eight hundred and seventy seven at the yearly rent of Eight pounds and subject to the covenants by the Lessee and the conditions by and in the said Lease reserved and contained **And whereas** after divers mesne assignments and acts in the law ultimately under an Indenture dated the twenty fifth day of June one thousand eight hundred and ninety six and made between Jemima Wilson of the first part Eliza Whitmore of the second part and the Vendor of the third part the premises became and are now vested in the Vendor for the residue of the term granted by the recited Lease **And whereas** the Vendor has agreed to sell the premises comprised in the recited Lease free from incumbrances to the Purchaser at the price of Three hundred and eighty pounds **Now this Indenture witnesseth** as follows: (1) In pursuance of the said Agreement and in consideration of sum of Three hundred and eighty pounds on or before the execution of these presents paid by the Purchaser to the Vendor (the receipt of which sum the Vendor hereby acknowledges) the Vendor as Beneficial Owner hereby assigns unto the Purchaser **All** the premises comprised in and demised by the recited Lease **To hold** unto the Purchaser for the residue of the term granted by the recited Lease and at the rent and subject to the Lessee's covenants and conditions by and in the recited Lease reserved and contained and henceforth on the part of the Lessee to

A typical early 20th century indenture. Decide whether you are going to list such illustrations in the preliminary pages of your book.

research, or your attitude towards the whole business. You could let this stand as an introduction to your book, or you could write an introduction in addition to, or instead of, a preface. Frequently a preface is followed by the name or initials of the author, together with a place and a date. This allows not a few authors to give the impression that they are forever lounging around writing books or prefaces in Bermuda or somewhere equally exotic, and that they are in the habit of referring to 4 August as St Nicodemus' Day as a matter of course. If you insist on playing this game, do avoid Pancake Day or April Fools' Day as the date for a preface, won't you?

- Acknowledgements.

Do be careful here. Either mention almost no one, or mention absolutely everyone. It's rather like sending out invitations to a wedding; most people will accept it if you explain that you plan to have a very small family wedding; what they won't happily accept is a situation in which friends of yours, whom they consider no closer in friendship to you than they are, receive an invitation if they don't. If you go for comprehensive and detailed acknowledgements, do try to miss no one out. If people buy a copy of your book, knowing that they have helped you in a significant way during the research or the writing, they may go straight to the acknowledgements and be exceedingly irked if they haven't been publicly thanked. Who can blame them? Everyone loves to see his or her name in print (no one more than family history authors), and a cynic might say that every person you mention in the acknowledgements will mean at least one firm sale for the book once it's published. The only safe thing to do is to collect the names of those you will acknowledge as you go along; eventually you can go back over your old correspondence and pluck out any names you might have overlooked. You'll probably end up thanking certain people even though their contributions have been fairly minimal – just because you think it would be a nice thing or the right thing to do, and would give the named person real pleasure. The whole thing is a minefield, so do take it seriously. Acknowledgements for illustrations used can be incorporated in your main list, or given separately.

- List of subscribers.

If you've launched your book by way of collecting advanced subscriptions, then a cheap and effective way of thanking subscribers for their confidence in you is to print a list of their names – either at the front of the book, or at the back. This is a time-honoured practice, and the subscribers' lists of books published in previous centuries can make fascinating reading. In what order do you place the names? An alphabetical list would seem to be an eminently sensible device, but sometimes names appear in the order in which their subscriptions were received. If your subscription copies are numbered, then you would usually put the appropriate number against each person's name. Books published in a 'limited edition' are often highly prized by collectors; just remember, however, that a short print-run limited edition may simply indicate that the author or publisher, rather strapped for cash, is making a virtue out of a necessity!

- Introduction.

Your introduction will be written last of all. Yes, really! You cannot possibly know what you're introducing until you've written it first. If you sit down to write a family history and struggle over the introduction at the outset, you'll probably get frustrated and disheartened. Leave it until the end.

You may have had some general thoughts about family history or about the writing of a family history as work has progressed; in the introduction, try sharing these thoughts with your readers. The deeper I became mentally and even emotionally involved in the process of writing my own family history, the stronger grew the odd but not unpleasant feeling that my ancestors almost seemed to be at my elbow as I wrote about them. Thus it was that I used the word "eerie" in the opening paragraph of my introduction:

> *The canonization of Oedipus as the patron saint of family historians is long overdue; his quest for self-knowledge through an unravelling of the mysteries of his origins is essentially the same as that undertaken in a more modest way and with less*

harrowing consequences by thousands of 20th-century family researchers. Genealogy is, of course, a subject of enormous fascination whichever family we might be investigating; yet there can be something especially moving and almost eerie about tracing our own direct ancestry, warts and all.

In 1995 my cousin Donald Titford from Bath published *Moonrakers in my Family*, his account of various branches of the Titford family not covered in detail in my own book. Donald is as prone to a touch of philosophical pondering as I am, and his introduction opens like this:

Most stories start at the beginning and finish at the end. A family history is different. It starts in the middle and ends when the author decides to cry 'finis'. Its true beginning is lost in the mists of time and the end has yet to come.

Your introduction will no doubt be different again, born of your own reflections as you think back upon what will probably have been a long and even exhausting process of writing the story of your ancestors.

Why not use part of your introduction to deal with topics which wouldn't seem to fit naturally anywhere else? Might this be the place to examine the geographical occurrence of the family name at different periods in time, or to present some ideas as to the origins and meaning of the surname?

- The main text.

At last your story appears – the bulk of the book, and what the whole thing is all about.

Give careful thought to your chapter or section headings. Do they encapsulate the information which follows? Will you print them in large bold type? Are they phrased in a consistent way? There's no point in having one chapter entitled Thomas of Norwich, while the next one is worded differently, reading something like: The Story of William of Swaffham.

Will you use subheadings within chapters? Will you print them in bold type or italics? Will you place them outside the main text within a wide margin (a favourite ploy in centuries past, now rarely used)? Don't use only one subheading in the first chapter, but twelve in the second. Always aim for consistency. Will you indent longer quotations within the text? Will you print them in italics? Whichever decision you make, stick to it and be consistent. It may look as if a finished book which you buy in a shop is professionally arranged and presented as if by magic, but its professionalism will be the result of a great deal of careful attention to detail.

Number your pages. Anyone who wishes to quote from your book, or to refer to it for specific information – or to use your index – will need to have a page number reference. Make life easy for others! Each number may be placed centrally at the top or bottom of a page, or – very commonly – at the top right-hand corner of each right-hand page and at the top left-hand corner of each left-hand page.

Let page one be on the right-hand side. It's a time-honoured practice that the first page of the main body of your text should start on a right-hand page, and be numbered as page one. Thereafter all right-hand pages will carry odd numbers, all left-hand pages will carry even numbers.

As noted earlier, you could begin your numbering sequence on the page immediately following the title page. However, I would commend to you the suggestion I made earlier – namely, that you consider using lower-case Roman numerals for the earlier prelim pages, letting your first main text page be number 1.

• Conclusion.

A good conclusion will draw all the threads together; it may summarise the family story in a few sentences, or it may define a few themes that have been running through the book. It will take some careful thought before you write a conclusion, but it will be well worth the effort.

• Addenda.

You may well not need to make use of addenda, but if you have discovered some information which is vital to your story at a stage when it is simply too late to change your text, you could off-load this vital material in an addendum. The alternatives would be not to mention it at all, or perhaps to rewrite large sections of text. Remember: you won't stop discovering vital information just because you've written a book!

- Footnotes.

Footnotes. The very word suggests that these will appear at the foot of each page, referred to by way of small numbers (usually in "superscript" as your word processing package would term it) in the main text. In truth, you probably will need notes of some kind, but grouping these together at the end of each chapter or at the end of the book is much easier to handle than placing them at the bottom of each page. Not quite so handy for the reader, but much more readily arranged by the writer. You don't really want to use notes at the foot of the page, do you? Supposing that you add or subtract a paragraph or two at some stage, and the page divisions have to change accordingly. Where are you then? It can get complicated.

What exactly will you put in your notes? Some or more of the following:

o References. If as family historians we are to be taken at all seriously as "proper" historians and scholars, we do need to refer precisely to our sources. Heaven forbid that we should lay ourselves open to the charge levelled by Margaret Stuart, author of *Scottish Family History* (Genealogical Publishing Company, 1978 reprint of a 1930 original) at those who write what she calls an "anecdotal family history":

> *This is frequently the work of a lady. It lacks, as a rule, a sufficient number of dates and almost always lacks references.* (p. 16)

Phew! Avoid falling into such a category at all costs!

If you've quoted from a book, give the author and title of that book, the edition (if relevant), the year of publication and the page number(s), like this:

W.B. Stephens, *Sources for English Local History*, 3rd Edition, 1994. p. 63.

To get a fuller idea about the use of bibliographical abbreviations such as "op. cit." (from the Latin, *opere citato*), meaning "in the work already quoted", or "ibid" (from the Latin *ibidem*), meaning "in the same book, chapter, passage, etc", look at the footnotes to some scholarly works, or have a good close read of *Writing Local History: a Practical Guide* by David Dymond (Bedford Square/NCVO, 1981).

If you've quoted from a manuscript, either state that it's one in your possession or give the exact call number if it's a public document, like this:

Settlement Certificate, 10 March 1723/4. SRO DD/LW/18.

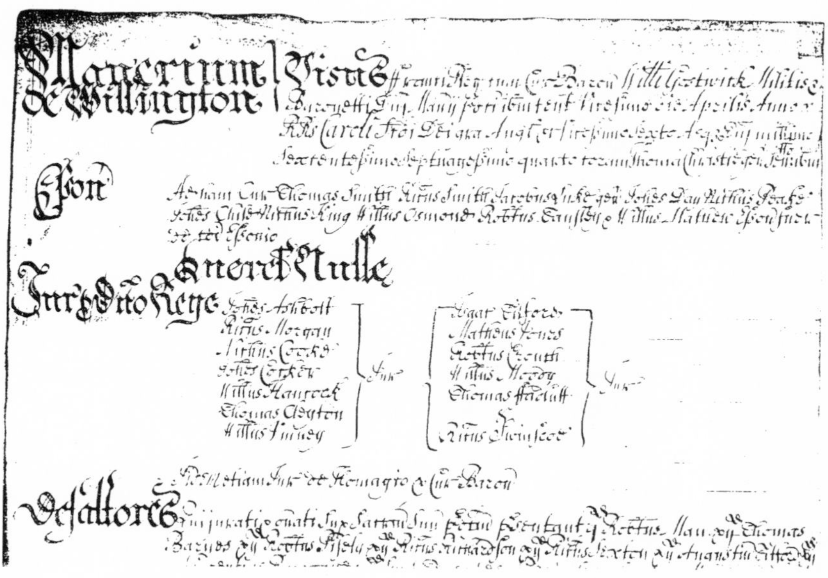

Manerium de Willington

Visus

Esson

Juratores pro Rege

Affeatores

Manor court proceedings, Willington, Bedfordshire, 1674 – make sure you state where such documents are to be found.

This refers to a document held by Somerset Record Office. To provide references in this way is both scholarly and also courteous. It shows that you haven't invented what you've been saying, and it allows anyone else who is interested to go back to the original source to see what they make of it. I must say that every time I acquire a new volume in the *Victoria County History* series, the footnotes are the first thing I look at; I want to know what original sources the editor has unearthed!

o Further family notes. It's important not to clog up your text with material which might be of interest to readers, but which is ultimately a side-issue that would interrupt the main flow of the narrative. Relegate such extra material to your notes (or to an appendix). Here you can, if you wish, say something about the ancestry of related or distaff lines – that is, those of women who marry into the main family with which you are dealing.

o Conjecture. There will be times when you are still uncertain about some key facts or vital relationships. Henry's birth has not been registered, yet you assume that he is the eldest son of John. Then there seem to be two contemporary Thomases, probably father and son, and a number of references might relate to either man. What do you do? It's best to decide upon one possibility which you find most convincing, and to stick with this in your main text. Meanwhile, in your notes, say quite honestly that there is a degree of conjecture here. The general rule is never to use conjecture on any serious issue without noting the fact. It simply isn't fair to your readers or to yourself to present hypothesis or conjecture as fact.

• Appendices.

I won't say that appendices are a dumping ground, exactly, but they do provide an excellent opportunity for you to include material in your book without its having to clog up the main text and interrupt the flow. In this sense, they're rather like expanded footnotes.

During your research you may have transcribed a number of

wills and/or probate inventories, for example. You probably won't want to include these in full in your main text, so you can relegate them to an appendix. You may have other lists or transcripts that can be dealt with in the same way. Number your appendices and, unless they're very short, use a new page for each one. Where necessary give some indication in the main text that an appendix contains expanded or extra information.

- Bibliography.

You may have read several books which you've found to be relevant to your story, or you may have consulted only a few. Either way, it's a good idea to list them in a bibliography, however brief. This will show that you've done some reading around the subject, and will point your keener readers to sources they might like to consult for themselves. The usual conventions for a bibliography are:

○ List the books by surname of author, alphabetically.
○ Put the author's surname first, then his first name or initials, then the book's title (in italics if you can arrange this), then the edition, if relevant, then the name of the publisher, then the year of publication (put "n.d." for "no date" if this is not specified). Here is an example:

Steinberg, S. H. *Historical Tables, 58 BC – AD 1961.* 6th edn. (Macmillan, 1961).

By all means classify the bibliography if it contains a large number of titles (for example: London; Hertfordshire; Kent; General). Treat pamphlets in much the same way as books, and if you wish to include a separate list of manuscript sources you have referred to, be sure to give the call number, like this:

Churchwardens' Presentments to the Precentor of Salisbury, 1617. WRO D25/12.

This example refers to a document held in the Wiltshire Record Office.

Try not to use a bibliography to show off your erudition and the breadth of your reading! If a book has been useful and relevant, include it; if it hasn't, exclude it.

• Glossary.

We spoke earlier about the fact that a certain number of your readers may find the world of family history a strange one, full of words or references which are unfamiliar. One way of making life easier for such people is to provide a brief glossary – make it an appendix if you like. Spell out what an "admon" is, explain the Hearth Tax, Hardwicke's Marriage Act, a removal order and a bastardy bond; say when the 19th century censuses were taken, unravel the mysteries of the IGI. This should help your inexperienced readers make sense of what you're saying, and you may well feel that it's preferable to use a glossary for this purpose rather than explaining unfamiliar terms in the main text as you go along.

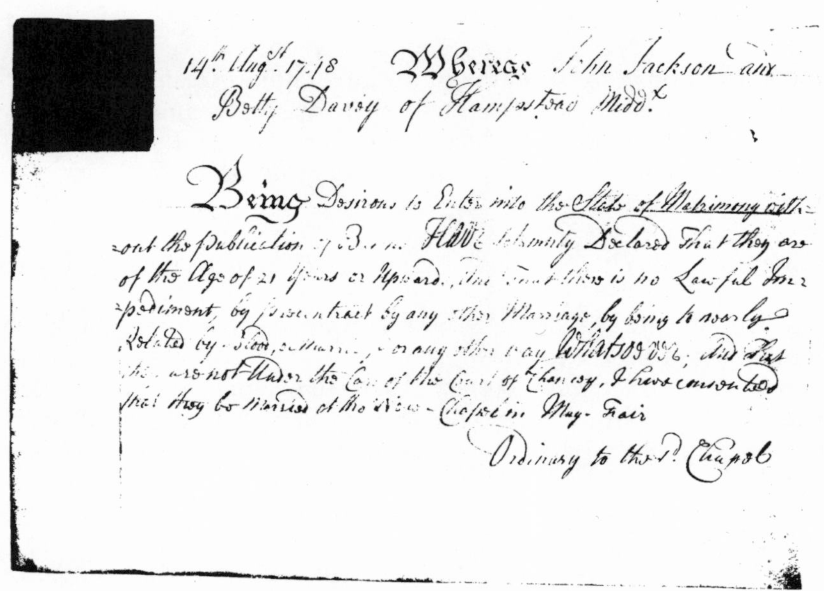

14th Augst 17.48 Whereas John Jackson and Betty Davis of Hampstead Middx

Being Desirous to Enter into the State of Matrimony without the publication of Banns Have Solemnly Declared That they are of the Age of 21 Years or Upwards, And that there is no Lawful Impediment, by precontract by any other Marriage, by being nearly Related by Blood, or Marriage or any other way Whatsoever; And that they are not Under the Care of the Court of Chancery, I have consented that they be Married at the New-Chapel in May-Fair

Ordinary to the sd Chapel

A marriage licence for a clandestine marriage in 1748. You may have to explain certain terms for inexperienced readers.

• Index.

We must work on the assumption that an index to your book is highly desirable. Some book reviewers will slate any publication that doesn't have one. That seems rather unfair, given the time and effort necessary to compile such an index, but family historians should know better than anyone that the usefulness of a book to other researchers is increased a hundredfold if it carries an index.

There are good indexes and bad indexes, full indexes and sketchy indexes. Unless you employ someone else to do the indexing for you (and that's always a possibility), you'll have a laborious task on your hands. You can use small record cards, scraps of paper or a computer for the task. Many word processing packages will alphabetise entries after a fashion, and you can tidy up the loose ends later. Use a database if you like. Either way, you can't compile your index until the book is in an advanced stage of completion; you must be sure that the pagination of the book (you will number the pages, won't you?) is finalised before creating an index that refers the reader to specific pages.

You might be ambitious enough to want to compile a full index of names, places and subjects (the old Index Nominum, Index Locorum and Index Rerum beloved of earlier writers), arranged separately or in one alphabetical sequence, but you might be happy to settle for an index of personal names only. If so, many of your index entries will refer to individuals with the surname of the family featured in the book. There's really no need to repeat the surname for every entry, but where there are people with the same Christian name, do distinguish these in some way – by adding the person's dates in brackets, for example, or by giving them a place-name designation. Many massive volumes have been written on the art or science of indexing, so don't get too worried about it all – just remember that you are trying to make your book user-friendly.

• The back end.

At the end of your book, the "back end" as I might unofficially call it, you will have some space to fill if you wish to fill it. Do remember, however, that using every available blank space in a book can make it look cluttered and can so easily detract from any classical dignity it might otherwise have achieved.

The spaces theoretically available to you are:
On a softback book or a hardback book with no dustjacket: the inside rear cover and the back cover.
On a hardback book with a dustjacket: the rear inside flap of the dustjacket and the rear cover of the dustjacket.
You could use all or some – or none – of this space productively if you so wish. You might decide to include some of the following elements, but do try to be guided by the "minimal clutter" principle:

o A brief summary of what the book is all about. This could certainly be of use to potential readers, and if you add a few commendatory remarks about your own work, singing its praises and saying what a vital contribution it makes to the fund of human knowledge, you'll have thus produced a "blurb", as they call it in the publishing trade.

o A biography of the author. This needn't be long and needn't be deadly serious. Include a photograph if you like. Such biographies are frequently seen on the inside rear flaps of dustjackets.

o Source of supply. It's certainly prudent to inform readers where copies of the book in question may be obtained, if not from the publisher (whose address would normally appear on the back of the title page). Perhaps some kind person has offered to take a stock of the books and post them out to customers? Give a name and address, and also a telephone number if you wish.

o Advertisements. This may be your one and only book, but if you've published others, then don't miss a golden opportunity to advertise them for sale, together with prices. Indeed, you could use some of the space available to you to advertise almost anything. You might be happy enough to accept some financial help from a retail business or an organisation in exchange for advertising space. If not you might, for example, care to advertise your paid services as a genealogist or record agent or a searcher in indexes you have created.

o The price of your book. This should be indicated somewhere, normally on the back cover (or on the inside front flap of a dustjacket). Not all publishers now choose to print a price in this way, but if inflation does take a sharp upward turn and you still have stocks of your book left unsold, you can always use stickers showing a higher price if you feel you must.

You may not wish to fill the back cover/back of dustjacket with text, but would rather leave it blank. Alternatively, you might wish to use it for an extra illustration, or you might choose to carry over the front-cover illustration in a "wrap round" fashion. This can be most effective, and is not uncommon.

- Illustrations.

If you possibly can, you ought to consider embellishing your text with a variety of illustrations, the reproduction of which should prove no great difficulty either to a publisher, or to you if you publish your book yourself. Illustrations can usually be made to occupy as much or as little space on a page as you wish. Some merit a whole page to themselves; others don't. It's certainly not ideal to bunch all your pictures together in just a few pages – this was the method commonly adopted by publishers earlier this century, when they had to use glossy art paper for maximum quality of reproduction. Ideally your illustrations should punctuate your text, and be placed as close as possible to the reference which is made to them in the story. Do give each illustration a caption which explains what it is, and maybe its significance, too. Tell the reader what he or she is looking at. Place your caption underneath the illustration if possible; if not, put it on the opposite page (or even the page before or the page after, if you really have to), making it clear that it refers to the page opposite, the page preceding or the page following.

You might consider using any or all of the following kinds of illustrations:

o Facsimiles of manuscript documents.
These can add a great deal of atmosphere to any family history. You might immediately think of using facsimiles of parish register entries, wills, manorial records and the like. Do pause for a moment, though: to begin with, you'll have to get permission to use such illustrations, and in any case, why not use your book to act as a showcase for documents which you have in your own private possession? In theory anyone could go to a record office and look at a specific parish register entry; but without visiting your house, they may never get to see the family bible, original letters, certificates or family notes which you have in your family archive. If you do use facsimiles of documents held by various public repositories, you'll need written permission; many record offices won't charge you for this, but a few will. In any case, you should refer to the original holder of such documents in your acknowledgements.

If possible, try to feature documents which are visually striking as well as historically interesting. You may well have far more illustrations than you can possibly use, so you'll have to prioritise somehow. A handsome-looking removal order with a royal coat-of-arms at the top will make a more striking illustration than an extract from some legal proceedings or other written out in spidery handwriting. An extract from an overseer's accounts book penned by someone with good calligraphic skills will look more arresting than one written by some poor unfortunate suffering from the palsy.

o Facsimiles of printed documents or books.
You might like to use newspaper obituaries, extracts from commercial directories, printed broadsides, posters, theatre programmes, Masonic Lodge cards, Loving Memory cards, poll books and the rest.

o Photographs.
You might use photographs of your ancestors (or of yourself and your own family), singly or in groups. If a picture is worth a thousand words, what better way to bring your family history alive than to arrange for grandmother to be staring out of the page at us, be she ever so stern and on her dignity, or wearing a

34445

We Granville George Earl Granville Viscount Granville Baron Leveson, a Peer of the United Kingdom of Great Britain and Ireland, a Member of Her Britannic Majesty's Most Honourable Privy Council, Knight of the Most Noble Order of the Garter, Lord Warden of the Cinque Ports and Constable of Dover Castle, Her Majesty's Principal Secretary of State for Foreign Affairs &c. &c. &c.

Request and require in the Name of Her Majesty all those whom it may concern to allow

Mr. Francis Dusterwald, a naturalized British Subject (1884) travelling on the Continent

to pass freely without let or hindrance and to afford him every assistance and protection of which he may stand in need.

Given at the Foreign Office, London, the 14th day of May 1885.

Granville

SIX PENCE

Signature of the Bearer

Visually striking documents such as this 1885 passport can add atmosphere to a family history.

dimply smile as a result of the photographer's urgings ("Say 'prisms' – Good! Say 'prunes'. Even better!").

If you feature a group photograph, do your best to name as many people in it as you can. If you are lucky enough to have any 19th or earlier 20th century photographs, these will probably be sepia prints of the *carte de visite* type, or perhaps a larger cabinet portrait. In many cases it is possible to date photographs with some degree of accuracy. The photographic process used may be one clue: is it a daguerreotype? An ambrotype? A tintype? There are some excellent books available on this very subject, including *Family History in Focus* by Don Steel and Lawrence Taylor (Lutterworth Press, 1984) and *Dating Old Photographs* by Robert Pols (Federation of Family History Societies, 1992). Maybe you can narrow down the date of a portrait in your collection by a close examination of the clothing being worn by both men and women? A very useful book in this regard is *Fashion à la Carte 1860–1900* (catch the pun in the title?) by Avril Lansdell (Shire, 1985). This may well help you to establish an earliest possible date for any particular style of clothing, but be aware that great aunt Jemima may have carefully kept a favourite dress for many years, only getting it out of the moth-balls when a visit to the photographer's studio was being arranged. By the time her photograph was taken, her dress may have been well out of fashion. If a male ancestor is wearing a uniform, new avenues of research could be opened up for you. Was he in the army? Which regiment? Was he in the police? In which town? Was he a member of a Masonic Lodge or a Friendly Society? Even the accoutrements of the photographer's studio (a chaise longue or a rustic stile) may be a clue to dating.

Another way of arriving at an approximate date for a photograph is to locate the photographer in a Victorian or Edwardian commercial directory. This can tell you that a certain photographer was at a location given on your *carte de visite* portrait at a certain date, which will be a start. Maybe he had been at a different address six years previously, but had moved again three years later? You're narrowing your date down, though do remember that the information included in any directory of a specific date could well have been collected in the

Charles Frederick Titford (1856–1899). A carte de visite dating from the 1870s – detective work is sometimes necessary on photographs.

year preceding that date. If you are interested in London photographers, then much of the work has already been done for you – look at *A Directory of London Photographers 1841–1908* by Michael Pritchard (Photo Research Books, 1994), with its exceptionally useful alphabetical listing. The Royal Photographic Society has published a series of directories of photographers, and for Australia I can strongly recommend *The Mechanical Eye in Australia (Photography 1841–1900)* by Alan Davies and Peter

Stanbury (Melbourne, Oxford University Press, 1985). Don't get too excited by a note on the back of a photograph that says something like: "Negatives kept, and copies may be had at any time. No.778546". That photographer or his successors may still be in business – but the odds may well be against you.

It's certainly possible to reach far back in time through photographs. I have a *carte de visite* portrait of my great-great grandfather, taken in the 1860s. He was born in 1814. You may even find a photograph taken at the same period which shows an old person who was born in the 18th century. Eerie, isn't it?

Not all photographs were taken in a formal studio setting. You might have a picture of your grandfather's shop in the High Street, hung with game birds, with grandad and his assistant outside, looking especially impressive for the cameraman. What a lovely period piece that would make! Photographs of people doing things are often more intriguing than mere studio portraits – there's great uncle Fred failing to catch a beach ball thrown by his nephew Billie! As a general rule, Victorian and Edwardian pictures will be more formal and posed than those taken in later years – especially since the advent of the ubiquitous and cheap Box Brownie and its successors. Could our ancestors have guessed that we'd now be filming a family wedding on a camcorder? They might be turning over in their graves even now . . .

The most frustrating thing about old photographs, be they loose or in a family album, is that so few of them will have been identified. Rarely, it seems, has anyone thought to write the name of the sitter on the back. That's no surprise really, is it? If grandfather turned the pages of the family album to show the photographs to a friend or relation, he would need no *aide memoire* as to the identity of each person featured. It's only once grandfather has died, taking his memory to the grave with him, that you're left staring at a bunch of people who might as well be total strangers. They're probably all relations – but who? You may not be too concerned at not knowing the identity of the dog shown on page three – but who is that splendid Victorian lady with the pince-nez, set within a large oval on the first page? I've never tried a visit to a spiritualist to seek help in this regard, though it might be something you would consider? Meanwhile, where you *can* identify individual portraits, at least make sure that you write an identity in pencil on the back of each. Don't let the same mistake be made all over again.

When my paternal grandparents had to move into a residential home in the early 1960s, their house in North London had to be cleared quite quickly. So it was that my parents, under pressure to get things done and with little enough time for sentiment, gave the family photograph album to the junk man. I've had to clear houses hurriedly myself since then, and so I understand why so many potentially interesting artefacts get thrown away. It was in the 1980s that a chance telephone conversation with my aunt on family matters led to her remarking that she had a duplicate family album which she'd rescued from my grandfather's sister. "I was about to throw the photographs away and try to sell the album," she said. I put Auntie on hold until I could get down to London to recover the album – and it was a real gem. Now when he was a child, my father had regularly been sat down on his father's knee for a special treat to be shown the hallowed photograph album, and each person would be identified. Glory be – my father still remembered the names of almost all the people in his great aunt's album, including that of his great grandfather – and so we were back to a man born in 1814. It had been a very close shave, and I do sympathise with those of you who have never had, or only just missed preserving, a family photograph album.

A word of warning won't come amiss here. Late in 1994 my friend and one-time neighbour from London, Alan Tew, wrote to me concerning a new book he'd just received, edited by a cousin of his wife's called Gordon Wilson. One of the photographs in the book caught Alan's eye. Here were two attractive young girls, holding an ornate board bearing a verse:

I want my album to contain
The old familiar faces
Of all my dear and valued friends
All in their proper places.
I hope you'll not intrusive find
The request that I now make:
A portrait true of every friend
I ask for friendship's sake.

Gordon's caption for the photograph read: "Beppie (left) and Eunice (right), about 3½ years difference in age". Now Alan Tew was taken aback by all this; he had no relationship whatever with the Wilson family, but he had the self-same photograph in his own family album – and had lovingly identified the two girls as "Louise and Kate Dove". You may be ahead of me already on this one, but the answer here is that the young girls were neither Beppie nor Eunice, neither Louise nor Kate, but a pair of models used by the manufacturer of the photograph album to pose for a kind of sample picture to set the ball rolling, family and friends being exhorted to offer their own contributions to the album. I featured this story in *Family Tree Magazine* in March 1995, and further correspondence confirmed the fact that other readers also had a copy of this sample photograph – or one very like it – in their own albums. So beware – if experienced family historians can wrongly attribute photographs in this way, anyone can. And by the way, be aware that many photographs of national dignitaries found their way into family albums; think twice before writing "great grandfather Harry Jones" on the back of a portrait of William Ewart Gladstone!

Another warning, just for good measure. When my paternal grandfather was very little, his mother dressed him up like a girl, and he had long flowing hair. It was always said that she had wanted a girl, and so subconsciously she tried to turn the poor little lad into one. This is far from unique; do think twice before "sexing" the photograph of a young child. You might get it wrong!

If you do possess old portrait photographs, then, you will regard them as special and valued treasures. It would make sense to have the most precious ones copied – especially if you plan to hand one over to a printer or publisher for inclusion in your book. Faded photographs can often be given new life and greater contrast in this way. By all means copy such photographs yourself using a single lens reflex camera with extension tubes or close-up lenses, and consider doing so outdoors in natural daylight for simplicity's sake. See a very useful article on this subject, "Copying treasured photos" by Bill Rees, in the January 1996 edition of *Family Tree Magazine*. If you'd rather have the job done professionally, look out for advertisements in *Family Tree Magazine* and in other magazines and journals; many photographers specialise in this area of work, and will probably offer a better and more sensitive job that your local chemist's shop.

So much for photographs of people. You might also want to feature local views, or photographs of schools, churches, cars, bicycles, charabancs. You may also be able to locate photographs of local events which would have featured prominently in the life of a community – even if your ancestors aren't actually shown. Carnivals, Temperance Society marches, Sunday school outings, war victory celebrations – all were favourite topics for photographers. Contact a local record office or a local history society and see what you can come up with. And can you get a copy-photograph of the ship aboard which great uncle Ernie went to Australia by writing to the National Maritime Museum in Greenwich?

You may decide to take some photographs yourself, especially if some of the old family homes or haunts are still extant. There may be a monumental inscription or two that you'd like to feature. It's not the easiest thing in the world, taking a photograph of a gravestone or other monument that will reproduce well in a book, but do persevere if you can. See if different light conditions at different times of the day or at different seasons of the year will give you a better result. Failing all else, why not make a detailed drawing, showing the wording clearly in full?

o Paintings, engravings, etchings, sketches and drawings.
You may have some nice paintings or drawings of family relevance tucked away somewhere? You may not have a portrait in oils, and no one may have bequeathed you a charming portrait of great grandmother on a miniature, but can you find a sketch *of* Auntie Ada, or one drawn *by* Auntie Ada? Maybe there is an autograph album somewhere with such treasures in it? Do you have drawings or paintings of the family home or its immediate neighbourhood? Sketches of family pets? Family cars?

If you're on the look-out for engravings or etchings of local views or even local celebrities with a family connection, you may perhaps find some in older books or pamphlets which would reproduce well and not involve you in any infringement of copyright.

In any case, do you have the skills to enhance the text with a few pictures of your own? Drawings of a church or a house? Even a conjectural picture of what you believe your great-great-grandfather might have looked like (based, perhaps, on photographs of his sons which are in your possession)? Some authors like to include a cartoon or two in order to add a touch of light relief to their book. That's up to you!

Do remember that not all facsimiles or other illustrations you

If you have the skill, why not use drawings of your own?

use need name or feature anyone in your family specifically. They could simply add a flavour of the environment in which your ancestors moved. They could simply suggest that great grandfather would have signed an apprenticeship indenture like this, worn a jacket like this, lived in a street like this, gone to a school like this, travelled in a tram like this, shopped at a shop like this, fought on a battlefield like this.

o Maps.
There's nothing quite like a good detailed map for bringing alive the area in which your ancestors lived and moved and had their being. Try and obtain one for the appropriate period or periods if you can, and identify the places where various family members were settled if you can find this out. You can buy facsimiles of the earliest Ordnance Survey maps, though you might get more joy by visiting the appropriate record office and asking about town maps, tithe maps, enclosure maps and estate or manorial maps. There are some truly magnificent examples around if you strike lucky. If not, why not attempt a simple uncluttered map of your own?

It might suit your purposes better to include a map covering a wider field – a county or a region, for example. This will give a broader context, and you may want to reproduce a regional or a national map on which you have marked family migration patterns or major concentrations of the family surname at certain periods.

o Pedigrees.
For the purpose of illustrating your book, it would seem ideal to make use of drop-line pedigrees – that is, where brothers and sisters are linked by horizontal lines, and vertical lines separate each generation. These can be of enormous value to the reader who needs to have a clear picture of family relationships. Ideally you would draw one overall simplified pedigree covering the entire family story, then a series of more detailed ones featuring two or three generations at a time. Space these out throughout the text if you can; if not, group them together at the end. Arrange your pedigrees sideways on a page if that helps, or even paste a folded pedigree into the back of your book – a device

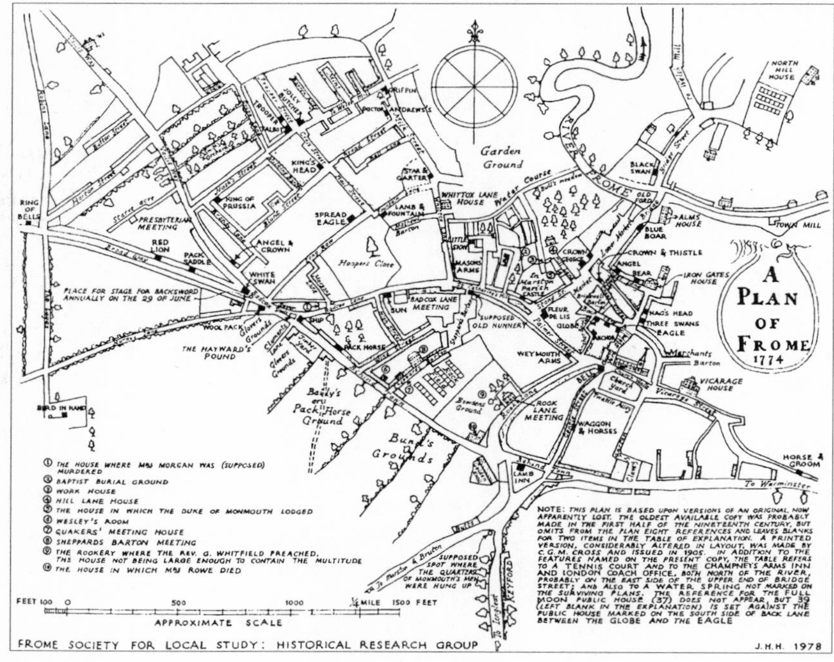

Contemporary maps bring an area alive for the reader.

used, for example, by Anthony Wagner and Antony Dale in *The Wagners of Brighton* (Phillimore, 1983). The conventions governing drop-line pedigrees are very simple, and you'll have little enough difficulty in finding some examples. A marriage is indicated by an equals sign (=), and a short vertical line coming down from a married couple then meets a horizontal line at right angles along which the children are placed. Most people start at the left with the eldest child, then work along to the right, but sometimes you'll find all the males grouped together on the left, in order of birth, followed by all the females. Usual abbreviations would include "bap" (baptised); "mar" (married); "bur" (buried) and any others you believe would be unambiguous. A favourite on older pedigrees (but still useful) is "d.s.p." (from the

Latin, *decessit sine prole*, meaning "died without issue"). Don't forget the often-used and deliberately vague term which you can attach to dates, "circa" (abbreviated to "c"), meaning round about, approximately. A great boon!

You'll no doubt also need to decide how to present dates which appear as "Old Style" in original documents. Before 1752, each year began on Lady Day, 25 March, not on the first of January. A document dated 12 February 1691 is only 1691 in Old Style dating, as it is known. In modern terms, its date is 1692. The usual convention is to yoke both years together using an oblique stroke, thus: 1691/2. Don't just convert an Old Style date to a New Style date without any warning – or someone will come along and add yet another year to it!

If you have highly-developed calligraphic skills, you could make a wonderful job of your pedigree charts; if not, be as neat as you can, or use one of the many computer programmes on the market.

If you have drawn up a set of truly exhaustive and comprehensive pedigrees which might threaten to overwhelm the text, you could follow the lead of Francis Warneford and Elisabeth McDougall, whose book entitled *An English Family through Eight Centuries: the Warnefords* (1991) has a supplementary volume called *The Warnefords: a Lineage*, featuring an extensive collection of family pedigrees.

o Heraldry.

If armorial bearings have been associated with your family, it would be a crying shame not to feature these somewhere in your book. Have you inherited some silver or china bearing a crest, a bookplate, or a seal matrix ring? Be careful, though: we all know about "bucket shop" heraldry, don't we? This practice was rife in the 19th century, and is making a comeback in the later 20th century. There you are, quietly minding your own business in a large shopping mall, and you come across a desk manned by a smiling salesperson with a computer. You give your name, you pay your fee, and out rolls a fancy scroll or certificate telling you that someone who happened to have the same surname as you happened to have used a particular coat of arms – rightfully or not. It's all harmless fun, though coats of arms were not granted

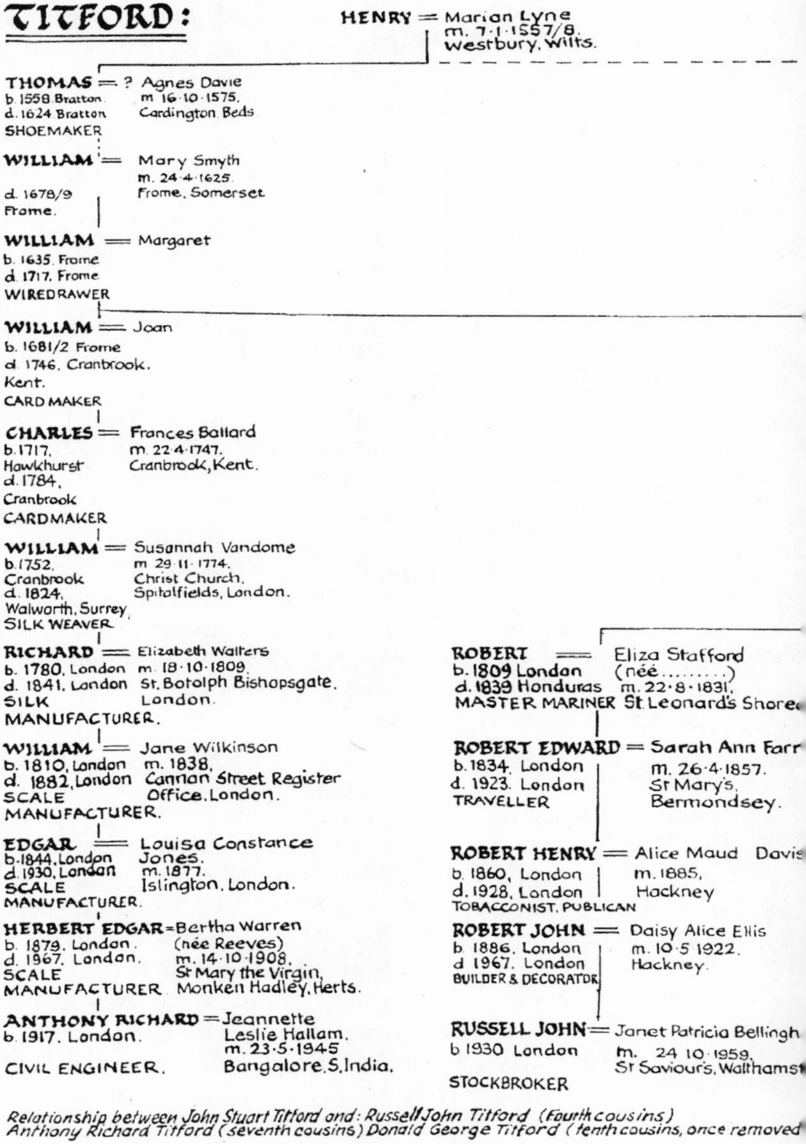

TITFORD:

HENRY = Marian Lyne
m. 7·1·1557/8.
Westbury, Wilts.

THOMAS = ? Agnes Davie
b. 1558 Bratton. m 16·10·1575.
d. 1624 Bratton Cardington. Beds
SHOEMAKER

WILLIAM = Mary Smyth
m. 24·4·1625.
d. 1678/9 Frome. Somerset
Frome.

WILLIAM = Margaret
b. 1635. Frome
d. 1717. Frome
WIREDRAWER

WILLIAM = Joan
b. 1681/2 Frome
d. 1746. Cranbrook.
Kent.
CARD MAKER

CHARLES = Frances Ballard
b. 1717. m. 22·4·1747.
Hawkhurst Cranbrook, Kent.
d. 1784.
Cranbrook
CARDMAKER

WILLIAM = Susannah Vandome
b. 1752. m 29·11·1774.
Cranbrook Christ Church.
d. 1824. Spitalfields, London.
Walworth, Surrey
SILK WEAVER

RICHARD = Elizabeth Walters
b. 1780. London m. 18·10·1809.
d. 1841. London St. Botolph Bishopsgate.
SILK London.
MANUFACTURER.

WILLIAM = Jane Wilkinson
b. 1810, London m. 1838.
d. 1882, London Cannon Street Register
SCALE Office. London.
MANUFACTURER.

EDGAR = Louisa Constance
b. 1844. London Jones.
d. 1930. London m. 1877.
SCALE Islington. London.
MANUFACTURER.

HERBERT EDGAR = Bertha Warren
b. 1879. London. (née Reeves)
d. 1967. London. m. 14·10·1908.
SCALE St Mary the Virgin,
MANUFACTURER Monken Hadley, Herts.

ANTHONY RICHARD = Jeannette
b. 1917. London. Leslie Hallam.
m. 23·5·1945
CIVIL ENGINEER. Bangalore. S. India.

ROBERT = Eliza Stafford
b. 1809 London (née.........)
d. 1839 Honduras m. 22·8·1831.
MASTER MARINER St. Leonard's Shore

ROBERT EDWARD = Sarah Ann Farr
b. 1834. London m. 26·4·1857.
d. 1923. London St Mary's.
TRAVELLER Bermondsey.

ROBERT HENRY = Alice Maud Davis
b. 1860. London m. 1885.
d. 1928. London Hackney
TOBACCONIST. PUBLICAN

ROBERT JOHN = Daisy Alice Ellis
b. 1886. London m. 10·5·1922.
d 1967. London Hackney.
BUILDER & DECORATOR

RUSSELL JOHN = Janet Patricia Bellingh
b 1930 London m. 24 10 1959.
St Saviour's, Walthams
STOCKBROKER

Relationship between John Stuart Titford and: Russell John Titford (Fourth cousins) Anthony Richard Titford (seventh cousins) Donald George Titford (tenth cousins, once removed

Drop-line pedigrees are ideal for illustrating family relationships.

MAS = Sarah Lacey
3. Frome m 5·2·1732/3.
1. Frome Frome, Somerset.
MAKER

RLES = Elizabeth Carpenter
'49 m. 9·7·1770.
2 Frome Frome, Somerset.
SEMONGER

JAMIN = Elizabeth Hasted
6 Frome m. 24·1·1808
6 London All Hallows by the
DER Tower, London

JAMIN = Elizabeth Augusta
4 London Josephine Parkes.
9 London m. 22·3·1846.
RSMITH Christ Church, Watney
Street, London

IAM = Mary Ann Keziah
London Parkes.
London m. 2·3·1872.
St James, Clerkenwell,
AVER London.

RY JAMES = Margaret Willox Archibald.
5 London m. 8·9·1902
7 London Arundel Square Chapel,
BEATER. Islington, London

IEY HORACE = Ethel May Buckler
04, London m. 26·6·1930
ANY St John's, Queens Drive,
TARY Finsbury Park, London.

N STUART
London.
E LECTURER

HENRY = ? Joan Henton
m. 29·4·1582
Bratton, Wilts.

WILLIAM = Rachel
b. 1600.
Sutton Veny, Wilts.
SHEPHERD

WILLIAM = Emary
b. 1622/3.
Wylye, Wilts.
d. 1670/1, Wylye

WILLIAM = Anne Bath
b. 1654, Wylye m. 6·10·1684.
d. 1730 Wylye Wylye, Wilts.

WILLIAM = Elizabeth Taylor
b. 1693, Wylye m. 19·1·1720
d. 1762, Wylye Wylye, Wilts.
SHEPHERD

WILLIAM = Christian Duke
b. 1725, Wylye m. 22·4·1751.
d. 1806, Wylye Teffont Evias, Wilts.
SHEPHERD

WILLIAM = Elizabeth Oram
b. 1755, Wylye m. 11·4·1779.
d. 1837, Wylye Fisherton Delamere, Wilts.

JAMES = Mary Leach
b. 1780, Wylye m. 23·8·1802.
d. 1862, London Fisherton Anger, Wilts.
AGRICULTURAL
LABOURER

WILLIAM = Anne Eliza Brenchley
b. 1817, Wylye m. 5·3·1838.
d. 1880, London St Pancras, London
UNDERTAKER

MAURICE = Eliza May Bennett
b. 1847, London m. 22·6·1875.
d. 1908, London St. Lawrence's Aberdeen
UNDERTAKER Park, Islington

PERCY MAURICE = Emily Hannah McLaren
b. 1876, London m. 13·11·1912
d. 1968, Sunbury-on-Thames St Pancras, London
UNDERTAKER

DONALD GEORGE
b. 1925, London
REAR-ADMIRAL, R.N.

to families as such – they were granted to individuals for their own use, and descend thereafter through all male offspring. In Scotland, such descent only passes through the eldest son in each generation; younger sons have to "matriculate" the arms of the head of their house with a suitable heraldic "difference", which is assigned according to specific rules. So there is no such thing as a Bloggs Family coat of arms. Nevertheless, if your surname is a rare one, and you find armorial bearings listed under this name in Burke's *General Armory* or some such publication (still no guarantee that the arms were borne as of right), it would be worthwhile trying to get a pictorial representation of the arms, even if your text makes it clear that those arms have only the most tenuous link with your own branch of the family. The commoner the surname, the less likely it is that any listed armorials for that name will have any family connection with you at all.

Heraldry is a wonderful art – and even a science – in many ways. Any given arms can be reduced to a written description called a blazon, using many words of French origin. So the arms attributed by the *General Armory* to the Davers family of Rougham, Suffolk, for example, are described in the following terms: "Argent, on a bend gules three martlets or". The colour, metal or fur of the background, called the "field", comes first, "argent" meaning silver in this case. "Gules" is red, "or" is gold, and a "martlet" is a bird rather like a swallow, but with the legs extending only as far as the thighs and finished off with two tufts. Three of these in the Davers arms are spaced out on a "bend", which is a band formed of two parallel straight lines running from the top left-hand corner of the shield to the bottom right-hand corner. Now the true fascination of heraldry lies in the fact that any heraldic artist can be as imaginative as he likes when converting this blazon into an illustration; providing he represents the features listed, he has a great deal of artistic licence.

If you find a blazon for a coat of arms you would like to feature in your book, either learn about the subject from books (there are many on the market), try to find a heraldic artist, or contact the Institute of Heraldic and Genealogical Studies in Canterbury, the College of Arms in London, or the Court of the

Lord Lyon in Scotland. If you want a fine quality illustration made from a blazon, this will not be particularly cheap: heraldic art is a specialised subject, and its practitioners are experienced professionals who will produce a work of real merit.

You may well want to spare yourself the expense of reproducing a coat of arms in full colour, in which case help is at hand. If you wish, you can "trick" the arms, which involves the use of abbreviations for the colours, metals and furs – "O" for or, "A" for argent, but "B" for blue, the English translation of the French azure. You simply write each abbreviated term neatly and inconspicuously on the arms in the appropriate place, using a short line to point to the feature concerned if necessary. Another method used to indicate the various armorial tinctures has come to us courtesy of Petra Sancta, a 17th-century Jesuit writer on armory. His system of hatching is very frequently seen, not just on black and white armorial illustrations, but on armorial silverware and even on carvings in wood and stone. The Petra Sancta method represents the tinctures using lines, dots, or other hatching. Closely-spaced vertical lines represent gules, horizontal lines indicate azure, a close pattern of small dots is used for or – and so on. So it is possible to include a black-and-white armorial illustration in your book which may not have the impact of full colour, but where those colours are at least indicated in an unequivocal way.

If you don't want to be accused of going over the top, I would caution against letting a full-colour armorial adorn the front cover or front dustjacket of your book unless the arms are yours by inheritance or have been granted to you personally.

In a rather less grand vein: if you can't come up with any heraldry which is relevant to your family (and this won't be an uncommon experience), why not make up a collage of family autographs by way of an interesting illustration for your book?

So much, then, for what I hope has been a comprehensive list of all the elements that could make up a book. Remember again that it's a matter of "could", not "must", and that you also have at least some discretion regarding the exact order in which you place the components that I've listed.

PUBLISHING YOUR FAMILY HISTORY

●●●●●

The day will dawn when you have finally completed your book in all its aspects. The family history itself is now as good as you can make it, and you've added a number of extra elements comprising both text and illustrations. Congratulations! You've reached that critical stage that lies "between product and production" (to borrow a phrase used by Ian Templeton in his book *Biographics: publish family history; inexpensive ways to do it yourself* (Piker's Pad, 1982, p. 68)).

This is a good time to pause and take a breath before you carry on. Is there anything major that you've omitted? Are there any changes that you need to make now, before it's too late? Whether or not you've asked friends or relations to read samples of your work as you've gone along, now could well be the time to hand your script to someone you trust, asking for their honest opinion and for any suggestions for changes. Yes, I know you won't really want to alter anything now, but a calm and honest assessment at this stage could prove to be of great long-term benefit. If a friend doesn't point out a flaw or two now, a reviewer may well do so later!

A cursory glance at a handful of "published" family histories will give you some idea as to the range of these that exists. At one extreme will be a modest A4 publication consisting of a few sheets run off on a stencil duplicator, "cyclostyled" as we used to say, held together with a couple of staples. At the other may be a product which has clearly cost someone (the author or his sponsor) a tidy fortune, no expense spared. I have one such in front of me as I write. As I intend to offer this item for sale in a future book catalogue, I'll quote you my full catalogue description of it:

KILCHURN HERITAGE: A magnificent boxed set of items, produced with no expense spared, to the highest standards.

o A fine box ($19\frac{1}{2}$" × 15"), black morocco-effect simulated leather, smart tartan lining, gold-blocked with the words "Kilchurn Heritage" on the front.
o A fine quality facsimile reprint of "THE BLACK BOOK OF TAYMOUTH with other papers from the Breadalbane charter room", originally printed privately (Edinburgh 1855) for the Marquis of Breadalbane for private circulation to be given as presentation copies to friends and relations. xxxviii, 443pp. Large quarto, all edges gilt, black morocco-effect covers, bevelled boards, tartan endpapers; fine plates, nine in full colour, a black and white view of Kilchurn Castle and a portrait of Sir Duncan Campbell of Glenurchy.
o "KILCHURN HERITAGE: THE HISTORY" by Anthony Kamm and Rennie McOwan. 1986. 65pp. Bound as "The Black Book" (above), with several fine colour photographs and a full-colour pedigree of the Earl of Breadalbane.
o A cylinder, black morocco-effect to match, containing a large photographic print of Kilchurn Castle and a full-colour pedigree of the Earl of Breadalbane.

A remarkable publication, no. 463 of a limited edition, produced as a labour of love and no doubt at enormous expense.

I shudder to think what this grand and glorious family history item would have cost to produce; unless you've just come into a legacy or are prepared to take on a debt that you might be paying off for years, this kind of thing is probably not for you. Will you aim for something rather more modest?

By the time you've slaved over your book for a considerable length of time, proof-read it and added all the necessary extras, you may well feel that you have no energy left to publish it yourself, and be tempted to let someone else take all or some of the strain. Do be aware, however, that whichever publishing option you choose finally, much of the work involved can be done by no one but you. So be prepared for quite a lot of concentrated effort!

What are your choices now? You can adopt one of the following strategies:

- You could hand the entire book over to a publisher.

- You could take your completed book to any printer you can find who will offer you reasonable terms for a short print-run.

- You could prepare the book ready for publication, then hand it to a reprographics shop which will produce copies by means of photocopying and may also bind them for you.

- You could be your own publisher and printer, duplicating and binding copies of the book yourself in a form that you find acceptable.

FINANCING YOUR BOOK

It's not just a question of how much effort, time and skill you can put into the production process yourself; another crucial consideration at this point is the amount of finance you can raise to get things off the ground. It's clear that carrying out every stage of the production yourself will be the cheapest option, while using a publisher will be the most expensive, unless – and this is unlikely for the history of an individual family – he will invest some of his own capital in the venture. Publishing is no different from any other human enterprise: if you want high quality, and if you want someone else to spend his time and apply his expertise, it will cost you.

How will you finance your book? Consider the following:

- Pay for it entirely yourself, with or without a loan of some kind.

- Persuade other family members to share the financial burden with you. This could be distant cousins at home or abroad who have a particular interest or who are as keen to see the family history in print as you are. You may have a parent or an uncle or aunt who would be persuaded by an argument that ran: "Look, you've always said that you'd leave me a bit of a legacy in your will; wouldn't it be a good idea if you were to make a small donation now towards the publishing of this book? That would bring pleasure to you, to me, to the kids and to other members of the family." You'll know better than I do whether such arguments – which seem to me to be very reasonable – would cut any ice with your nearest and dearest. Certainly some parents feel they would rather see the smile on the face of their children or grandchildren in this life than have to imagine such a smile from the other side of the grave.

• Find a wealthy sponsor. Shakespeare and many another great author did it, so why not you? You may have contacted that fabled rich cousin living in America, or had some correspondence with a distant relative who made a fortune from his biscuit factory. Could they help out? Would a well-known company bearing your distinctive family name and with some distant relationship feel inclined to help you publish a quality book which they might even use as a promotional aid?

• If your family history features one particular locality very strongly, perhaps some individual or organisation in that place will help out in some way?

• Offer the book to subscribers in advance of publication. Now we're away from pipe dreams into a very viable and commonly-used alternative with a long history behind it.

Once your book is written, and before you've spent too much money on its production, prepare an advertising flyer or leaflet which extols the virtues of your product. State how the book will be bound (you could offer softback and hardback alternatives at different prices), approximately how many pages it will have, what kind of illustrations it will contain. Invite anyone who reads your leaflet to subscribe at a reduced pre-publication price which they should send in advance direct to you or to someone who may do the job for you. Quote an overall price

St Ethelburga, Bishopsgate – illustrations from old books liven up the text and could help to 'sell' the book to a local sponsor.

including postage and packing, not forgetting that good quality padded mail bags are not cheap! Anyone interested should give their details on a tear-off slip and send the money without delay. You must specify the pre-publication price, then, but needn't be exact about any final published price – "Approximately £15" would suffice. There's no point in tying your hands at this stage. Give an expected publication date and also a closing date for your offer – not too close, but not too far away, in case people leave your leaflet lying around and then forget about it. Say that the names of subscribers will be printed in the book if and when it is published, and ask the subscriber to specify how he or she would like this entry to read. You can number subscribers' copies if you wish – that does make them feel rather special and exclusive. Some generous souls may want more than one copy, each naming a different member of their family. You'll probably wish to say that you consider this book to be an important contribution to the history of the family, but that publication in this form will be an expensive undertaking, and will be dependent upon a sufficient number of subscribers coming forward.

All this presupposes that you've decided which form of publication you'd ideally like to go for and that you've costed it accordingly. If you're going to take the trouble to solicit subscriptions, you'll probably have opted to use a publisher, or a printer at least. If the subscription strategy fails, you can fall back on cheaper methods of production.

Post copies of such a flyer to any relations or friends you can think of; if your surname is unusual, consider sending a copy to everyone of that surname you can find in telephone directories across the country and even abroad. If your book has featured one town or village very prominently, send a copy or copies to the local newspaper in case they can make a story out of it or feature it in some way. Some authors have produced a professionally-printed single-sheet flyer and paid to have one inserted in family history magazines or journals. This will cost you, of course, and you might decide that this was too large a financial gamble to take for your modest family history?

If the response to your pre-publication offer is healthy, you can go ahead and publish in whatever way you have decided, posting subscribers their copies as soon as you can. If the response is borderline, you may have some hard thinking to do. If very few people express an interest, you may simply have to reimburse the few faithful supporters and think again. It could well be that it's only once your subscribers have responded that you'll know whether you can afford to produce your book using one of the more expensive options open to you.

It wouldn't be unduly cynical to suggest that you might like to consider a publication date in November or early December; your book could be used as a very welcome stocking-filler by those who have gone for the after-shave Christmas present option more often than they have wanted to.

PUBLISHING OPTIONS

Once you have made a realistic assessment of the financial commitment you are prepared to make, you'll have a better idea of what publishing options are open to you. We'll now attempt to cover all the possibilities.

- Using a publisher.

Let's get the question of a publisher dealt with straight away. Do you really need one, and if you do, will he take the financial strain, or will he expect you to take all or some of it? Make no mistake, few if any printed family histories are going to make much of a profit for anyone. You could send a synopsis of your book to an established publisher, but you might well receive a rejection slip in return, or a request for a large sum of money to carry out what in effect could be a form of "vanity publishing". A publisher is in business to make money, not to dispense philanthropy; he's not there to make you feel happy, nor to publish a book that might be fun and not much else, or that might be intensely interesting to a mere twenty people. If your book doesn't look like a runaway winner, a publisher probably won't handle it, and if it looks as if it could be a sure-fire success, why not get most of the profit from it yourself? There is nothing quite so satisfying as seeing your book appear over the imprint of a well-known publisher (I was delighted with Phillimore's professional approach to the publication of my work on the Titford Family), but many books would never have seen the light of day if their authors hadn't taken the bull by the horns and published their own work themselves. Publishers are rather like lawyers – potentially excellent when you need them, but dispensable more often than you might think. A publisher will certainly take some of the strain, and should have the wherewithal to handle advertising, selling and distribution effectively, but even if you can convince him that your book is a good bet, he will also take a fair amount of the money, too. That's no cause for complaint – it's just part of the reality of the market place.

If you do use a publisher, he should make a distinction between that which he needs you to provide, and that which he will do for you. Ask him exactly what he wants from you; he'll probably be delighted to have your text on a compatible computer disk, and may tell you how you should present the illustrations and other bits and pieces that make up the final book.

• Publishing the book yourself.

Now let's suppose that you're going to be bold enough to handle the book production yourself. A few years ago we would have been talking about some very Stone-Age reprographic alternatives indeed, such as carbon paper, banda machines (a cheap and smelly process much used in schools at one time) or stencil duplicators – typically manufactured by Roneo or Gestetner. Carbon paper and bandas hardly seem appropriate for the task in hand, and if you've been planning all along to use a stencil duplicator, you'll have been busy cutting your stencils and correcting errors with a bottle of liquid that smells like nail varnish – unless you've decided to go up-market and use an electric scanner to copy text and/or illustrations onto a stencil. I remember the bad old days of ink duplicators. When I was about twelve years old, I produced a small local news-sheet in North London called the *Woodside Park Clarion*. Profits from the first two months' sales allowed me to buy an old second-hand flat-bed duplicator. You'd fit a stencil into the frame, then ink the whole thing using a roller. I thought I was king of the universe. How things have moved on since then!

It's more likely, isn't it, that you'll use a more modern reprographic method such as a photocopier, or will take your book to a printer specialising in short print-runs? Unless you take a computer disk to a printer and let him do the "typesetting" for you, you'll have to produce camera-ready copy – that is, text and illustrations which can be duplicated or photographed exactly as they stand.

As usual, there'll be a few aspects of the process to think carefully about. Here they are:

o Format.
I'm using the word here to refer to "landscape" format, in which the book has its shorter edge running vertically, and its longer edge horizontally, or "portrait", where the long edge runs vertically and the short edge runs horizontally. In other words, a landscape book has a short spine and wide floppy pages, whereas a portrait book has a long spine and feels tall. Of the two, portrait is by far the commonest. It feels right somehow. A particularly large landscape book, on the other hand, can be a librarian's or book collector's nightmare. It might end up being placed on the shelf with the spine at the top or bottom, to avoid the book protruding so far that it risks being knocked to the ground by every person who passes by. Landscape can work well for illustrations that have more width than height, and could be ideal for pedigrees. That being said, I'd strongly advise that you stick with the old familiar portrait format.

This might be the place to mention the fact that you could arrange your text into columns; indeed, you'll almost certainly have to if you use a landscape format. Reading a long line of text can be tiring and dispiriting. Most word processor and desk-top publishing packages will offer you the facility of creating columns: I use "newspaper columns" on Word Perfect for the production of my book catalogues, and it's simplicity itself to set up.

o Page size.
There seems to be little enough uniformity these days with regard to page size – just look at the books in your public library. It will probably suit you, for all that, to work with one of the standard metric paper sizes established several years ago by the British Standards Institution and with which British (but not American) readers will now be very familiar. A metric sheet referred to as "AO" would measure one square metre, but the sizes we'll come across in common everyday use will be A3 (420mm × 297mm), A4 (297mm × 210mm) and A5 (210mm × 149mm). If you prepare your camera-ready copy on

A4 sheets of paper, then the printer or the reprographic shop will be able to reduce it to a smaller size if necessary. If you intend to do your own duplicating, then most reprographic systems will be able to reduce your text percentage-point by percentage-point. There are fixed reduction ratios too, of course: if I instruct my photocopier to reduce an A4 original to A5, it will switch to a 70% reduction setting of its own accord.

You might decide to print or photocopy onto sheets which you'll then fold in half at the binding stage (for example, A4 sheets folded to make A5), in which case it will be vital to think carefully about where each page will be placed in the order of things. If you were producing a mere leaflet of eight numbered pages, for example, you'd copy pages one and eight on one side of a sheet, right and left respectively, with pages two and seven on the reverse; the second sheet would have pages three and six on one side, and pages four and five on the other. This might not sound complicated, but it can become so, believe me! It's probably best to make up a dummy book as a basis from which to work.

o Style and size of type.

You can have an enormous variety of options here if you use a computer with appropriate software. If you're using a typewriter, you may have a daisy wheel or a golf ball that can be changed to give you different typefaces – or you may have no choice at all, and will have to use the type that is standard for your machine whether you are typing text, notes or headings.

Any sophisticated computer software will offer you a range of fonts, that is, styles of type. These may be called Times Roman or Dutch or something else, depending upon the manufacturer; they may be serif, sans-serif, or utterly individualistic. Once you've chosen your style, you can choose the size – "point size" in the jargon. For everyday use I go for ten or twelve-point type, but if you intend to reduce at the copying or printing stage, you'll need to experiment. Twelve-point type on an A4 sheet reduced to A5 is rather too small to be read comfortably, so start off with a larger point size. If in doubt make your type size larger; this will mean that your book will contain more pages, but nothing could be worse than the thought of your readers struggling to read the text that you've slaved over so carefully for so long.

Of course your headings can be in larger, bold type; your footnotes or notes might be in smaller type; you can use italic or bold or underlining at will. Don't overdo it, though – this is a family history, not a type-founder's specimen book! I wouldn't contemplate using a gothic or "black letter" font (as used, for example, for the masthead of the *Daily Telegraph*); you may feel that this will give your book an olde-worlde feel, but it always looks rather precious, and some of the more extreme letter forms can be almost impossible to read!

Your computer software will almost certainly offer you options such as "proportional spacing" and "justified right margin". Proportional spacing will give your text a more pleasing appearance by allowing for different widths of characters. The letter "w", for instance, is wider than the letter "i", but would normally be allocated the same amount of spacing. With proportional spacing, the "w" is given more space than the "i", creating a more even and professional appearance. As to "justified right margin", if a margin is said to be justified, it means that your eye sees a straight line as it follows that margin down the page. The left-hand margin of any block of text will be justified (unless you have deliberately indented it) whether it's produced on a typewriter or a word processor. What a word processor (or an electronic typewriter) can do for you that a manual typewriter can't, however, is to justify the right-hand margin. Perhaps it is this feature that most enables computer-set type to resemble the real old-fashioned typesetting of the past. In the days of lead type, spacers had to be inserted to make the right-hand margin of a book or newspaper appear to be in a straight line as you looked down the page. Now all this can be done electronically. What magic!

Type style and size are largely a matter of personal choice. At least that choice is available to you if you have access to a computer and the appropriate software. I can't help thinking that a good classical serif face or font (that is, one where the letters have fine little lines finishing off the main strokes) would seem to be most appropriate for your journey into history.

Page number with even nos. on left-hand page

Facsimile illustration, reproduced with permission and with a frame

Portrait format, long edge running vertically

Generous margins, top, bottom and sides

Running title (or head)

190

MOONRAKERS IN MY FAMILY

Also they present William Titford Shepherd to the East end flo
for ffeeding his fflock of sheep on the Cowdown contrary to the Custo
of this Manor, he having been presented for the like default att
two last General Courts held for this Manor And that he hath incu
the penalty of v^s for so doing and they now Order that the s^d Shephe
shall not feed the said Cowdown with his said fflock contrary to the
said Custom under the further penalty of v^s for each default . and
so affeared

MANOR COURT OF WYLE. 18TH JUNE 1764
William Titford, Shepherd to the East End Field, is presented
(WRO 2057/M54)

his identity into the open but it had also persuaded the Court to emphasise that the Custom of the Manor applied to William Titford specifically – just in case he should consider that a free breakfast on Sunday and the skins of any dead sheep placed him beyond the Court's jurisdiction. The 'presentment' reads:

> 'They present William Titford, Shepherd to the East end fflock, for ffeeding his fflock of sheep on the Cowdown contrary to the Custom of this Manor, he having been presented for the like default att two last General Courts held for this Manor, and that he hath incurred the penalty of 5/–d. for so doing, and they now order the said Shepherd shall not feed the said Cowdown with his said fflock contrary to the said Custom under further penalty of 5/–d. for each default.'[13]

The Manor Court of Wylye was wasting its time. Once again William the Pauper completely disregarded the Court's judgement and continued in his wicked ways. The Earl of Pembroke's steward persevered, however, and the following year, at the meeting of the Manor Court held on 24th June 1765 – the anniversary of the baptism of William's dead son, James – William the Pauper was again presented. This time they spelt his name wrong!

> Also they present that William Tidford, Shepherd of the East end fflock of sheep, was presented and amersed at the last General Court held for this Manor for ffeeding his said fflock of sheep on the Cowdown contrary to the Custom of the said Manor, and because he has again been guilty of the like offence, they do therefore further amerse him five shillings.'[14]

By the time of the next meeting of the General Court of the Manor on 19th May 1766 the Clerk must have been praying for the rubber stamp to be invented. Already he had lost count of the number of times William the Pauper had been presented, but it didn't really matter since the Shepherd of the East end fflock continued to disregard the verdict of the Court and his annual presentment had now become a mere matter of routine. Nevertheless, at their meeting on 19th May 1766, the Manor Court conscientiously went through the motions of presenting William the Pauper as usual:

Title for illustration and a brief description of contents. Wilts. Record office document reference number

Number referring to notes at the end of the book

Quotation, indented and in small type

Main text in a classic serif typeface, not too large or small. Lines spaced neither too close nor too far apart

*A page from a family history (*Moonrakers in my Family *by Donald Titford 1995).*

o A running title.
Suppose that your book is called *The Grover Family*, and one chapter within it is entitled Down on the Farm. There would be three possible ways of presenting what is known as a "running title":

– At the head of each left-hand page the words The Grover Family would appear, ranged right (that is, lined up so that the last letter of the last word of this title was directly above the last letter of the last word of the justified right-hand edge of text). The right-hand page would be a mirror-image – that is, The Grover Family would be ranged left, the first letter standing directly above the left-hand edge of the main text.

Margaret Stuart, in her introductory essay to *Scottish Family History: a Guide to Works of Reference on the History and Genealogy of Scottish Families* (1930, reprinted 1978) is particularly dismissive of the "repeated book title" style of what she calls "headlines":

> *It is difficult to see what object this serves; congenital idiots do not as a rule read family histories, and it is difficult to conceive of any other class of persons who would require to be reminded at every page of the name of the book they were reading*. (p. 21)

So there. Let's quickly pass on, then, to more commonly-used alternatives:

– The left-hand page carries the book's overall title, while the right-hand page features the name of the chapter in question (Down on the Farm, or whatever).

– A third alternative would be for both running titles to read Down on the Farm, the chapter name.

The idea of both these last two options is that the reader can see at a glance exactly whereabouts he is in the book as soon as he opens it. I hesitate to say this, but it can also be a boon to anyone who photocopies (illegally or not) any part of your text; the photocopy will have the book or chapter title already there –

no need to write it on afterwards!

Incidentally, if you do use a running title, you'd normally omit it on a page which is all or largely illustrative – no point in letting it obtrude!

PREPARING A CAMERA-READY MASTER COPY

Once you've decided upon your format, page size, size and style of type and whether to use a running title or not, you'll need to set to and produce a master copy from which other copies can be made.

● Text.

Whether you'll be preparing your text pages using a typewriter or a printer linked to your computer, there are some basic guidelines you should follow:

○ Use one side of the paper only. There are two main reasons for this. First, if you make a significant error which necessitates retyping or reprinting, you won't have to redo the reverse side; secondly, any text which appears on the reverse side of a sheet may show through at the photocopying or printing stage.

○ Use generous margins around the edge of each master. The term "generous" is deliberately vague here, since you'd be wise to be guided by your own judgement, having looked at some examples of books which seem pleasing to you. A two-centimetre margin would be appropriate in most cases, though you should consider leaving a broader inner margin (for the "gutter" of the book, as it is called) to allow for binding. Set your typewriter or word-processor top, bottom, and side margins accordingly. If in doubt, leave more space rather than less. Nothing is worse than a page that seems to be too full of text.

○ Leave generous spacing between the lines of text. If you intend to reduce your camera-ready master at the photocopying or printing stage, experiment to see what the final result will look like. You may only have one or two standard line-space settings on your typewriter, whereas a word processing programme will allow you to enter a precise measurement to suit your needs.

o Avoid "widows" and "orphans". What on earth are they? A widow occurs when the last line of a paragraph appears at the top of the next page (lonely, bereaved and unloved, as it were), and an orphan is the reverse – when only the first line of a paragraph appears at the foot of one page, the remainder then continuing on the next page. Paragraphs are important building blocks in your text, and deserve better than to have their loose ends left lying around.

You may be preparing your text pages using a typewriter. If so, do aim for a good strong black print. A carbon ribbon is ideal, though more expensive in that it can be used once only.

If you're using a dot-matrix printer attached to your computer, again make sure that you have a ribbon which will give you a good clear black impression. If your ink-jet or laser printer is in good working order, there should be no problems; just make sure you aren't getting stray blobs of ink or toner on the copies.

- Illustrations.

If you're fortunate enough to be able to scan images into the word processing or desk-top publishing programme on your computer, you won't need any hints about the creation of master copies using paste and paper.

For those not so fortunate, let's think our way through the process of creating quality master copies of pages which consist entirely or largely of illustrations. You'll need good clear masters with plenty of contrast throughout; no copying process will improve upon a poor original.

Some of your illustrations may be straightforward enough (a portrait with a caption, for example) while for others you may be producing a collage of various elements, illustration and text, stuck on to a single sheet. Do bear this in mind: the important thing is that the final copies you make should be clear and clean, even if the master copy from which they are taken may look rather untidy. If you are pasting an illustration onto a blank

Name of

Reference No.	SIGNATURES OF CREW.	Age.	Town or County where born.	If in the Reserve, No. of Commission or R.V.3.	Ship in which he last served: State Name, and Official No. or Port she belonged to.	Year.	Date and Place of joining this Ship: Date.	Place.	In what Capacity engaged, and if Master, Mate, or Engineer, No. of his Certificate.	Time at which he is to be on board.
	1	2	3	4	5	6	7	8	9	10
1	James Field	42	Plymouth		"Cordelia"	1876	19.4.76	Plymouth	AB	20.4.76
2	W. Waring	34	L'pool		"Ireland Maid" Shields	1876	do	do	AB	do
3	Richard Brimblecombe	34	Plymo		Berkely Castle	1876	do	do	AB	do
4	David Reed	33	do		"Allerwal" Lpool	1876	21.4.76	do	AB	21.4.76
5	Carlos Torbe	27	France		"Salvador" Guernsey	"	17/10/76	San Francisco	Cook	17 Oct
6	Edward Evert	23	Ireland		"Arizona"	"	"	S.F.	AB	18 "
7	Francesco Pigassi	20	Austria		"Pepina"	"	"	S.F.	OS	18 "
8	[illegible]	20	London		"Australia"	"	"	S.F.	OS	17 "
9	C Clark	21	L'pool		Assaye	"	19/10/76	San Francisco	AB	20
10	John Welch	40	Waterford		J. Fitzpatrick	"	Do	Do	Do	20
11	Thos Richardson	34	Manchester		Assaye	"	Do	Do	Do	20
12	Robert Wilkie	34	[illegible]		Tidal Wave	"	Do	Do	Do	20
13	Daniel Sullivan	23	Greenock		Whistler	"	Do	Do	Do	20
14	William his X mark Bransfield	28	St. John's N.B.		St. Nicholas	"	Do	Do	Do	20
15	William [illegible]	40	Maine		Robert Dixon	"	Do	Do	Do	20
16	Charles his X mark Smith	25	Austria		C. of Phila	"	Do	Do	Do	20
17	William West	19	New York		first ship	"	21/10/76	Do	OS	21st
18										
19										
20										
21										

† If any Member of the Crew enters Her Majesty's Service, the Name of the Queen's Ship into which he enters is to be stated under the head of "Cause of leaving

* The necessary figure

A crew list of 1876 from the "Cartsburn" of Greenock. Even without expensive equipment quality master copies of illustrations can be made.

page (do use starch paste, Cow Gum or some other adhesive which doesn't stick too firmly, too fast, and apply it thinly), it may have straight edges, in which case you may need to use correction fluid (Tippex, Snopake or whatever) or a correction strip delivered by a "mouse" or some other dispenser to cover the edges of the illustration as they meet the background sheet. If you don't do this, you'll get unwanted lines caused by shadows. If you can do so, however, you should roughly tear the edges of the illustration you are pasting down; this will mean that those edges will usually be thinner, some of the paper fibres having been torn away, and should not cast shadows. In this case you won't need to use correction fluid providing you paste down the edges firmly. It really does work – try it! So I hope you can see what I mean by saying that an untidy-looking master may nevertheless produce good quality final copies?

o Use generous margins (two centimetres or so) for your illustration pages as for your text pages. Also allow breathing space within the page, if appropriate, especially if you're going to reduce the original in size. A crowded illustration page can look as disconcerting as a crowded text page.

You may choose to place some illustrations in a frame, leaving others to float free, as it were.

o You may create text which will appear next to an illustration (a caption, for example) using a typewriter or computer printer, but equally you may decide to use some form of instant transferable lettering such as Letraset. This comes in an impressive array of sizes and styles, and has revolutionized graphic art in the last three decades or so. If you use such lettering, do make sure that the letters are level and evenly spaced, and do be sure to use the backing sheet to buff them after they're in position. If you don't, whole letters or parts of letters will lift off and leave unsightly gaps. If you've made a mistake, try removing the offending letter or letters with sellotape.

o Borrow a trick from the graphic artists. If you need to establish a horizontal or vertical level for an illustration or for text accompanying an illustration, draw a line using a light blue pencil. A faint blue line will not be reproduced at the photocopying or printing stage, so can safely be left in place on your master. Here again, you needn't worry if a master looks messy, providing the final copies are clean.

o You can readily buy books full of copyright-free illustrations; simply photocopy the picture you want, reducing it or enlarging it if necessary, and stick it on your master where you need it to be. You could use such an illustration on a text page (next to a chapter heading, for example), but don't overdo it, or the whole thing will look tacky. There is usually a very wide range of illustrations in such books: Queen Victoria, shown head and shoulders; a crowded charabanc; a conjuror; the houses of parliament – and geometrical or floral designs and borders.

o The good news is that colour photocopying (like colour printing from a computer printer) is now well established – it may still not be a cheap option for you, but it could add real quality to your book. The bad news is that photographs, colour or black and white, will not photocopy well on a black and white machine unless they are particularly strong on contrast. As an experiment, try photocopying a photograph and then a picture from a newspaper. The copy of the photograph may well look murky and thoroughly uninspiring, while the newspaper picture could give you a clear, sharp copy. Why is this? It's because the newspaper photograph has been "screened", that is, reduced to a series of dots of varying density. If you take your book to a printer, he will screen your photographs before printing – it's one of the things you're paying him for. If you do intend producing your book using a photocopying process, it might be worth taking your photographs to a local printer and asking what he'd charge for providing you with a screened half-tone copy of each. If the price is reasonable, you can then use the screened copies for photocopying purposes.

MAKING COPIES OF YOUR BOOK

You now have your camera-ready master copy. What will you do with it?

Pause a moment: how many copies do you want? Would fifty suit your needs, or would you hope to sell five hundred or so? It's true that a commercial printer will only have to stand the cost of making a litho plate from your originals once, and that there is a unit-cost saving the more copies you have run off. Don't let this persuade you to have thousands of copies just for the sake of it, however!

Using a commercial printer at this stage is one option open to you, then; he can use your camera-ready masters (or your computer disks, for that matter) to produce a professional-looking final product. How printing technology has improved over the years! There are an increasing number of printing companies which are specifically geared up to produce short runs of books like yours. It seems like only yesterday (indeed, it was, in terms of the history of printing) that monotype printing machines would be clanking and chuffing away, or that type would be set in hot lead on a linotype machine. Authors would be presented with galley proofs to check for accuracy, and any error in a particular line of type would necessitate the resetting of the whole line. Too many author's corrections at this stage, and you'd be charged extra. Now most printers use computer typesetting and off-set litho printing machines; the technology has come of age.

There is no shortage of jobbing printers in today's world, so do shop around. Ask for a quotation for providing as many copies of your book as you will need, and enquire how much extra run-on copies would cost you. Don't necessarily opt for the cheapest quotation – have a look at samples of a printer's work to give you some idea as to the quality of his work.

If you decide that you can't afford to pay a short-run printer for his services, then other alternatives will need to be found.

You could run off copies of your book direct from an ink-jet or laser printer. Before you do so, try and have a look at an article entitled "*Publish your book: low cost or long life?*" by David Hawgood in *Family Tree Magazine* for February 1995 (pages 28–29). David has this to say:

> *There is far more difficulty at present with laser printing than photocopying. The toner from laser printing tends to set off if*

the printing is against a PVC cover, and laser printer toner seems very susceptible to acid in paper . . . I know from experience that some printing from ink jets is very susceptible to damage from damp, and some dot-matrix printer inks seem to spread in a damp atmosphere.

I would also commend David's article to you if you are interested in paper-life and in the cost of various printing and binding options as they stood at February 1995.

That brings us to the more obvious cheap-ish method of producing multiple copies of your book, namely, photocopying. Either you'll slave over a hot photocopier yourself, or you'll use your local reprographic shop. Maybe a local factory, office, school or college has a photocopier and would either run copies off for you at a price, or let you use their facilities (supervised or unsupervised) if you crossed a few palms with silver? It could be worth a try.

You may be able to choose which paper you use for the pages of your final book. By all means go for quality, even use some coloured paper if it seems appropriate, but don't go for a really heavyweight paper that the photocopier won't like. 80 gsm (grammes per square metre) is about the right weight to use for the bulk of your book. Pay extra for acid-free paper if you're really concerned about the durability of the final product.

Decide upon the reduction ratio, if any, you'll be working to. Experiment with this first just to be sure, and be aware that many photocopiers automatically revert to a standard setting if nothing seems to be happening for a while. If you stop for a chat and turn back to the copier, it might have wiped away your 70% setting and be back to 100%. Beware!

I could be wrong, but I don't think you'll particularly enjoy running off multiple copies of your book on any photocopier you can get access to. Never mind, you'll have to grit your teeth. Maybe you'll even use the copier in your local library, asking them for their key so that you can count the number of copies and pay for them all at one go, rather than stand there with a pile of 10p coins? In any case you're going to be embarrassed if anyone else is waiting, aren't you? In all conscience you'll have to cease your activities as the big-time publisher while a local chap runs off a copy of his tax return.

Photocopiers, like computers, have a life of their own. Some days they simply refuse to co-operate. As you get going on that most troublesome of all activities – back-to-back copying – they'll suddenly start coughing up warm, creased copies. Then there'll be a paper jam which necessitates a major operation deep inside the machine's guts to clear it. Then the toner will need replenishing and the used toner bottle will be full. Toner is a fearful thing. Little more than black talcum powder, it gets everywhere, sticks to everything, smudges your master copy, gets up your nose – and floats on water so that you can't flush it down the toilet even if you want to. Dreadful stuff. Are you sure you wouldn't rather use your local reprographic shop?

Once you have a huge pile of photocopied sheets, you'll then need to collate these into a number of copies with the correct pagination. Either try and find a mechanical collator (some photocopiers will collate as they print), or enlist the help of the family – get them walking round a large table, picking up sheets as they go. It will be a burden to do so, but you really ought to check each copy at the end to be sure that pages are neither missing nor repeated.

BINDING

From the cheapest to the most expensive, your binding options will be:

• Staples. As a matter of interest, printers refer to a stapled book as being "stitched", just to make life difficult for us all. You could place one single staple slantwise across the top left-hand corner or you could use two or three staples down the left-hand margin. If your book consists of large sheets folded down the centre, you should try to beg or borrow a long-arm stapler and staple down the centre of the folded sheet – this is known as saddle stitching.

Some staples do rust in time, alas, and can leave a brown stain and break the paper which surrounds them. This can be repaired if necessary, but if you use staples then your book may not have the healthy long life you might have wished for it.

As to covers, you could use single sheets of thin card front and back, with appropriate text and some illustration printed or photocopied on them. There are some pleasant linen-effect and laminated cards on the market, but try not to use anything too heavy for the job. It can be very effective to use a wrap-around card cover, glued to the spine.

• Loose leaf ring binder. This is a possibility, though a rather tame one, you might think. It's cheap, and pages can be added or removed at will. The normal choice would be a two-ring binder; punch holes in the pages of your book, open the rings, insert the pages, and close the rings. Stick a sheet featuring the title and an illustration on the front cover if you like, and also a spine title.

• Slide bar binder. This is the term I use for one of those round or triangular-shaped strips of plastic which is folded over in such a way that you can slide it up the spine to hold it firm. You'll need a slide bar of the correct length which opens far enough to accommodate all the pages. You can staple the pages before you use the slide bar, or not if you prefer. This is quite a pleasant form of binding, and fairly substantial unless someone drops the book and all the sheets tumble out! A simple title can also be stuck onto the binding if it's wide enough, though you might have to anchor this with clear adhesive tape, which is generally a highly undesirable product where any form of book binding is concerned.

• Spiral binding. You can create a fairly solid wire spiral binding for your book, but the more usual alternative is to use a lightweight coloured plastic spiral "comb". A simple machine (your local college or school may let you use one?) punches a series of slots on the edge of the book to be bound, and then fits the plastic comb into the slots. I must admit that this isn't my favourite form of binding: if there are too many pages, the book only opens with difficulty and the inner edge of pages can easily get creased, and the plastic comb can sometimes spring open and then close in the wrong way, leaving you with the tricky job of repositioning it. A spiral binding is serviceable but not very exciting, in my view. A quick glance through an office supplies catalogue may give you other ideas: "Channel" binding; "Post" binding, or the "Professional Velobinder" which "produces secure professionally-bound documents of up to 250 without heat or electricity. The pages are locked together with the unique patented binding strips . . ." It's not only family history authors who are looking for an inexpensive but durable and attractive form of binding, so do look around the world of office supplies and see what you can find.

• Thermal binding. Your local office supplies store will probably be able to sell you a thermal binding machine which uses heat to create a durable spine. A typical advertisement for such a machine would tell you that it "binds up to 500 pages in seconds" and comes complete with a cooling rack. What a relief! Thermal binders are designed primarily for office use, but might suit your needs very well.

• Perfect binding. If ever there was a misnomer, this is it. Perfect binding involves taking loose sheets and fixing them at the left-hand edge with adhesive. A cover is then wrapped around the entire book. This is a job that you'll need a local printer or bookbinder to do for you. It's far from perfect in the sense of "couldn't be bettered", but modern adhesives are a lot longer-lasting and flexible than they used to be. Soon after I'd entered the sixth form at school, I saved up my pocket money and bought a Penguin paperback edition of Graham Greene's *Brighton Rock*. The pages were far too heavy for the book, and were soon falling away from the brown adhesive of the binding in clumps. I was not amused. If you do use perfect binding, be sure to leave a generous inner margin; make sure the binder uses a strong and flexible adhesive – and make sure he uses paper which is light enough not to put strain on the spine every time the book is opened. There are now some very acceptable perfect-bound books on the market – handsome and apparently strong – so I'm being won over slowly.

• Case binding. This is the Rolls-Royce of binding, and will not come cheap. You might decide to have a few case-bound copies of your book produced – one for yourself and one for immediate family members – leaving the rest to be bound in a cheaper fashion.

If a book is case bound, it will be sewn with thread and firmly fixed within hard covers. A binder can produce a case-bound book from individual sheets of paper – something he probably does for university student theses at certain times of the year. This is a skilful job, but if he's honest, even a "craft" bookbinder will tell you that he'll make a series of holes near the inner edge of the sheets using an electric drill, and will then run a thread up and over, in and out of the holes. An electric drill – whatever next! The next stage will be to attach endpapers at the top and bottom, glue the spine, surround it with a strong cloth called mull, and then glue the book itself into the made-to-measure case which he's made of thick board and cloth. The book's title can be "gold blocked" onto the front cover and the spine as required.

That leaves the best-quality and most expensive binding of all, namely, the use of sewn sections – the style of binding used for centuries, long before the invention of electric drills. A section will start off life as a large sheet of paper on which various pages of the book have been printed in a specific order, some the right way up, some upside-down. This is known as "imposition". The sheet is then folded – once to make a folio, twice for quarto, three times for octavo, and so on through duodecimo and the rest, depending upon the number of folds made. Each set of folded pages constitutes a section or "signature"; all the sections will then need to be trimmed and sewn together to make the final book. The result should be a strong, durable product, easy to open, with a convex spine and a concave "foredge", as it is called. If you take your loose master sheets to a printer, he could use these to produce the large sheets necessary for sewn sections to be made.

Cover your case-bound book with a dustjacket, and you will have a quality product of which you can be proud and which should last for years to come. With luck it will look nice, feel nice and even smell nice. It'll leave a gaping hole in your bank balance, but you might feel that it's been worth it.

There is a fairly modern alternative to using a dustjacket as such. If you look at a number of books published in recent years, such as the Phillimore series, *Hatchments in Britain*, you'll see that instead of having plain cloth-covered boards, in effect they have a dustjacket glued to the boards and the spine, incorporated into the book and not separate from it. Laminated paper is frequently used for this purpose. This can look very handsome, and you should see whether a local printer or binder can offer you such an alternative. This is known in the trade as a 'cover for case' or 'self-covered' style.

MARKETING, ADVERTISING, DISTRIBUTING AND SELLING YOUR BOOK

You now have multiple copies of your book, printed and bound. They might be cluttering up your house or your garage, so the next imperative is to get rid of them and to get some cash in return. Let's move on to the next stage, as you become less of an author and publisher, more of a salesman.

- The selling price.

Whether you've launched your book by way of a subscription list or not, you'll have copies to sell. You'll need to establish a selling price – indeed, you'll already have had to do so before printing the price on your book. It's unlikely that you'll make a profit (especially if you were ever to cost your own time into the equation!), but presumably you'll also want to minimise your losses. Breaking even may be your wildest ambition. Do remind yourself at this stage that your book has been your very own creative venture, and that as such has probably given pleasure not just to you but to other members of the family, too. In that sense you've already had your reward; now you'll be keen that as many people as possible should read what you've written, especially if they might be distant cousins, previously unheard-of, who might contact you with priceless new information. With all this in mind, see if you can keep the selling price as low as possible. It's better to sell all the books you've had printed by offering them at a very reasonable price than to be left with a loft full of unsold copies which were too expensive for anyone to buy, and are now gathering dust. Don't forget that every book sold is potentially another book sold, in that a book acts as its own advertisement. Distant cousin Amy visits distant cousin Betty, sees your book on the coffee table, and immediately writes to you for a couple of copies. To some extent, the more you sell, the more you're likely to sell.

• Who to sell to.
Try as I may, I really can't avoid using the dreaded word, "market". There should be a market out there for your book – or rather, a series of markets. As they might say on a sales course, define your markets, inform them of your product, then sell to them. It makes sense. What markets will you have? Immediate family, wider family, friends, neighbours, libraries, interested genealogists or local historians, people living in a locality you've featured strongly, and so on.

• Advertising your book.
How do you inform your potential customers of the existence of your book? By word of mouth, by letter or FAX or E-mail, or by producing a flyer. Why not use the reverse side of the front portion of some spare dustjackets for this purpose? Certainly you should try to leave a few flyers lying around wherever you go (without being a litter lout), and you could even pay to have some sent out as inserts in relevant family history journals or magazines. You should also compose an informative and persuasive press release for appropriate newspapers or journals. Here you must give full details of the book, specifying a price (inclusive and exclusive of postage and packing both inland and overseas). Give your name, address, telephone and FAX or E-mail number. Decide upon a publication date and specify when this will be. Give the press release a title, and try to come up with a selling angle. You can see it now, can't you: the editor of a local newspaper reads your press release, sees that a family history will include text and pictures about his town, contacts you for a chat, asks if he can copy one of your photographs, and runs a feature which gives you a great deal of publicity and will cost you nothing. Even the editor of the newspaper covering

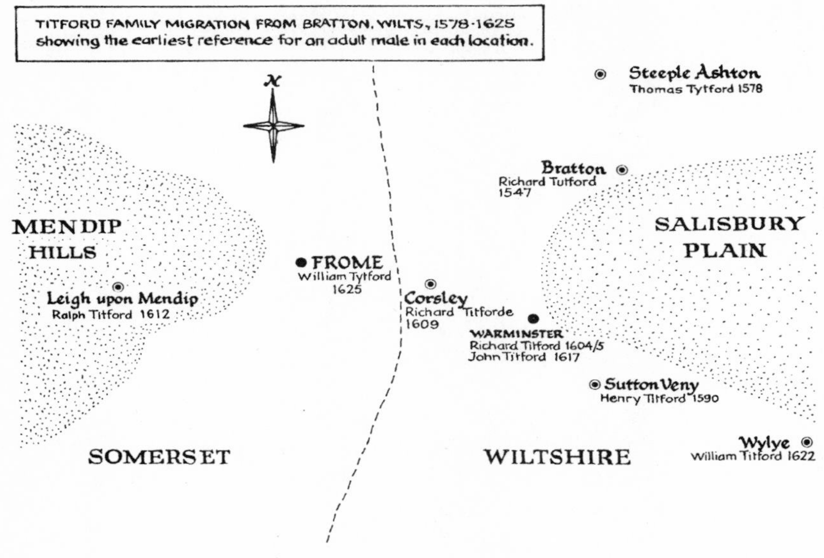

A family map can clarify migration patterns and show prospective buyers the area your story covers.

the area where you now live – miles away from your ancestral roots – may compose an article under the headline: "Local woman traces her roots . . .". An ounce of free publicity is worth a pound of paid advertising. Generally assume, nevertheless, that journalists are busy people: let your press release do most of the work for them, and don't be surprised if it appears in the newspaper exactly as you've written it. Why not send a press release to your local radio or television station, followed up by a telephone call a few days later?

I cannot overemphasise the importance of the judicious use of free copies. Give one book as a present to each of your nearest relatives and to those who have made a sterling contribution to the finished work. I'd go so far as to say that any copy of your book given away free will pay financial dividends in the long run. The person who receives it will feel grateful to you, others may see his or her copy and want one of their own – and everyone will generally feel warm and cosy inside. Goodwill will abound.

Not only that, but I do hope you'll wish to present a free copy of your book to an appropriate local library or record office. If you send a complimentary copy to the Society of Genealogists (14 Charterhouse Buildings, Goswell Road, London EC1M 7BA) for their library, you should also enquire whether they would consider reviewing it, or at least giving it a mention, in their *Genealogists' Magazine*. Do send a review copy to other family history and local history journals or magazines, not forgetting any Family History Society that covers the areas featured in your book. Reviewers are usually very kind and tolerant to authors of family histories; they will have some inkling of the work involved, they'll know how much the book means to you, and although they may have a few reservations, they'll normally praise you for having taken such effort. Make the reviewer's life a little easier: do produce a single sheet of paper which gives full details of your book, its price (including postage and packing, home and overseas), the source of supply and a brief synopsis of the contents, and tuck this into the review copy you send. Use one of your press releases for this purpose if you like. The review itself should generate sales for you, so please don't ask for your review copy to be sent back to you!

If you are unlucky enough to get an unfavourable review, your best bet is to keep a low profile. By all means write to the journal concerned to correct an error of fact in the review, but don't get into a slanging match. Let sleeping dogs lie.

• Selling and distributing your book.

So you've defined your markets, you've informed them of your book; now you've got to sell copies.

Why not throw a party to launch your masterpiece on the day of its publication? Organise one at home and invite all your friends and relations, or get some free food laid on in the village pub which is mentioned in your story, and drum up some local interest. Avoid certain times of the year like Cup Final or Election Day. Produce some posters and handouts, generally sound off a fanfare; this may be the first time your ancestral village has been featured so prominently in words and pictures in a book. Will the local publican sell some copies for you on commission, or will the vicar take a few on sale or return, pleased to receive a modest contribution to church funds? How about the local post office? Will the local Building Society manager give you a free window display? Can the town library help you publicise your masterpiece?

Let's assume, however, that most of the copies of your book will be distributed by post; families are now so widespread that many of your customers will live nowhere near you. Every book sold in this way will be a direct sale, and the full price will come your way. Don't be embarrassed about charging for packaging as well as postage – Jiffy bags don't come cheap! As soon as anyone else sells for you – be it the publican, the vicar, the postmaster, a local shop, a family history society, the Society of Genealogists, a family history magazine or whatever, you'll have to share the proceeds. A retailer as such would normally expect to keep a third or so of the cover price, though if the books are on sale or return you should try offering only 25%, and you won't get paid until the books have been sold. You may only feel this is worth it if a particular retail outlet can reach the parts you cannot reach. The vicar or the Family History Society may expect less of a cut, and here you must negotiate.

Normally you'd expect to sell quite a few books in the first few weeks or months, when it's all new and exciting, and when people with their ears to the ground hear the good news that your book is in print. Thereafter things will probably slow down to a trickle, perking up when a review appears, or when a copy bought by someone in Australia suddenly generates some interest down there. Eventually you may sell out. If you do, a week later some dear sweet cousin you didn't know you had will be on the phone, desperate to buy a copy. If only you hadn't done the hard sell on people who weren't really interested, or paid the retailer his 35% cut, you'd be better off financially and your new-found cousin would be happy. Too late! It's a good policy, then, to keep a reserve of a dozen copies or so, only to be sold or given away in very special circumstances.

Now let me share with you a spot of good financial news.

• Books are zero-rated for VAT. This isn't the same thing as saying that they are not subject to VAT: they are subject to it, but the rate (at the time of writing) is zero per cent. This means that you won't have to go through the paraphernalia of charging VAT and then reclaiming it if you're eligible to do so. Not only that, but if you're paying a printer to deliver *complete books* to you (and he may have sub-contracted parts of the production such as typesetting and binding to someone else), then his invoice should be free of VAT. A gentle reminder before he starts work might not come amiss. Why pay 17.5% extra if you don't need to?

• Public Lending Right. If your book is lodged with one or a number of libraries and is borrowed by a significant number of people, you deserve to make at least a small financial gain. After all, someone who might otherwise have bought a copy of your book may get to read it for nothing by using a public library. The rewards under the Public Lending Right arrangements won't make you rich, however. Payment is made at the rate of two pence per loan, the calculations being based on returns from a sample of lending libraries. To register and to have at least some chance of getting a few lots of two-pences, write to: Public Lending Right Office, Bayheath House, Prince Regent Street, Stockton-on-Tees, Cleveland TS18 1DF (telephone: 01642 604699).

A few years ago I was a co-author of a book on communication and media studies. The book seems to have sold extremely well, and every year all three co-authors get a royalty cheque from the publisher. Also, because the book is used extensively by schools and colleges, teachers are very prone to making photocopied class sets of portions of it. As a result, we also receive quite substantial regular payments from an organisation called the Authors' Licensing and Collecting Society of Isis House, 74 New Oxford Street, London WC1A 1EF (telephone: 0171 255 2034). This may well not be of interest to you unless your book finds a significant and ready market in educational establishments where the photocopiers seem to be whirring all day long.

Even your parents and grandparents are part of your family history! Here, the author's parents, Sid and Beth Titford, celebrate their diamond wedding anniversary in 1990.

CONCLUSION

●●●●●

Can there be an appropriate conclusion for a book which exhorts you to write a family history and to publish it if you possibly can? Certainly by now I hope you will have cast aside my mocking suggestion at the start of this book that you might find the whole thing all too much for you.

I've been gratified over the years to find that talks I've given at various Family History Society meetings have persuaded at least a handful of people to lay aside all procrastination and to start writing a book they'd long intended to tackle one day. My earnest hope is that some of the readers of this book may tread the same path. I do think it's important, and I do feel that you'd derive an enormous amount of satisfaction from doing it. Who knows, I may even have the pleasure of writing a review of your completed book one day? I do hope so.

ACKNOWLEDGEMENTS

●●●●●

The author is grateful to the following for permission to reproduce illustrations: the Greater London Record Office Ref. P91/LEN/1336 (p. 14); the Corporation of London Record Office Ref. CF1/2172 (p. 32); the Public Record Office Ref. RG5 4659. No. 3365 (p. 37); Marjorie Edwards of 48 Freegrove Road, London N7 (p. 65); the Marquess of Tavistock and the Trustees of the Bedford Estate, from a document in the Bedfordshire Record Office Ref. R Box 212. Willington III. 12/1–80 (p. 71); D.G. Titford, *Moonrakers in my Family*. Privately published, "Merry Hill", North Road, Bath BA2 6HD, 1995 (pp. 86 and 105); The Secretary, the Frome Society for Local Study (p. 88); Lord Pembroke and the Trustees of the Wilton Estate, from a document now held in Wiltshire Record Office Ref. WRO 2057/M54. (p. 105); The document illustrated on page 109 is Crown Copyright material from the Maritime Archive, Memorial University, St. John's, Newfoundland (Crew Agreement No. 26739, "Cartsburn", 7th April 1876), reproduced with the permission of the Controller of Her Majesty's Stationery Office.

The illustration on page 9 is from R. Phillips, *The Book of English Trades and Library of the Useful Arts* (New edition, 1823). The illustration on page 20 is from *Kelly's London Directory 1867*. The illustration on page 98 is from Walter Thornbury's, *Old and New London*, vol. 2, p. 162.

All other illustrations are from originals held by the author.

INDEX

●●●●●